D0252867

POT-BELLIED PIGS
and other Miniature Pet Pigs

Lisa Hall Huckaby

TS-181

DEDICATION

To Yetti and Sherpa, the two beautiful Himalayan cats who brought special light and love to life for both my husband and me... and to all the other noble creatures in the animal kingdom. Thank God for giving us humans the animals to share this earth with us.

Distributed in the UNITED STATES by T.F.H. Publications, Inc., One T.F.H. Plaza, Neptune City, NJ 07753; in CANADA to the Pet Trade by H & L Pet Supplies Inc., 27 Kingston Crescent, Kitchener, Ontario N2B 2T6; Rolf C. Hagen Ltd., 3225 Sartelon Street, Montreal 382 Quebec; in CANADA to the Book Trade by Macmillan of Canada (A Division of Canada Publishing Corporation), 164 Commander Boulevard, Agincourt, Ontario M1S 3C7; in ENGLAND by T.F.H. Publications, PO Box 15, Waterlooville PO7 6BQ; in AUSTRALIA AND THE SOUTH PACIFIC by T.F.H. (Australia) Pty. Ltd., Box 149, Brookvale 2100 N.S.W., Australia; in NEW ZEALAND by Ross Haines & Son, Ltd., 82 D Elizabeth Knox Place, Panmure, Auckland, New Zealand; in the PHILIPPINES by Bio-Research, 5 Lippay Street, San Lorenzo Village, Makati, Rizal; in SOUTH AFRICA by Multipet Pty. Ltd., P.O. Box 35347, Northway, 4065, South Africa. Published by T.F.H. Publications, Inc. Manufactured in the United States of America by T.F.H. Publications, Inc.

POT-BELLIED PIGS
and other Miniature Pet Pigs
By Lisa Hall Huckaby

Jarrett Scott and a trio of young—and energetic—Pot-Bellies.

ACKNOWLEDGMENTS

The author gratefully acknowledges the following, who willingly and graciously provided photographs, information, anecdotes, and/or various pet pig facts that assisted in the development of this book:

Linda Davison of Critter Corner Acres in Marion, Iowa

Flame Beller and her piggies, "Penelopy" and "Snorker," at Pigg-EE Palace

Betty Scott of Scott Ranch in Prescott, Arizona

Betty Beeman and her staff at The Pot-Bellied Pig Registration Service in Indiana

Sara Wright and her mother Jane

Dawn Roller of the Best Pets exotic pet store

Tom Aubrecht of Shallow Creek Exotics

Douglas O. Johnson of Star Exotics

We are thankful to the following photographers and contributors, whose photographs appear on the pages as indicated:

Flame Beller, 10, 28, 30, 70, 97, 103; Linda Davison, 36, 42; Isabelle Francais, 6, 12, 13, 23, 24, 57, 71, 72, 73, 83, 90, 93, 101; Michael Gilroy, 26, 29, 31, 32, 33, 35, 51, 53, 63, 64, 65, 68, 69, 75, 77, 78, 81, 84, 128, 133; Huck Huckaby, 14; Lisa Hall Huckaby, 20, 39; Half Mile Lane Exotics, 56; Douglas O. Johnson, 34, 37, 40; Lea Line Exotics, 38, 87, 110; Courtesy Lil' Porkers, Ooltewah, TN, "Winston," 44; "Winston" and "Twiggy," 46; Courtesy MGB Farms, 54, 55; Betty Scott, 8, 9, 15, 16, 18, 19, 21, 22, 27, 41, 45, 48, 59, 61, 66, 67, 89, 94, 99, 105, 108, 113, 121, 124; Judy Watson, 25.

Special credit to models Naomi Powell and Jessica Powell, who appear in photographs on pages 15, 22, 41, 45, 59, 61, 89, 94, 99, 108; Carrie Crosson, on pages 8, 19, 67, 105; P. Kiser, on 93; Julie Jondahl, 66, 125; Mario, 48; Kimberley A Nelson, 9; Jarrett Scott, 3.

CONTENTS

ORIGIN

THE VIETNAMESE MINIATURE POT-BELLIED PIG, ALSO CALLED THE CHINESE POT-BELLIED PIG, IS AN ANCIENT BREED. SOME CLAIM THAT TODAY'S

THE ORIGIN OF THE POT-BELLIED PIG

Pot-Belly is the progeny of pigs raised by Neanderthal Man and that it is a breed which has evolved unchanged for four million years. They are known to have originated in Southeast Asia and China as the descendants of Eurasian feral pigs. Originally they were domesticated as house pets and for food, as early as the tenth century.

In 3468 B.C. To Hi, the Emperor of what later became the People's Republic of China, scribed the existence of the Pot-Bellied Pig. He noted their small size and distinct wrinkles in what is considered to be the first book on the raising of pigs. Tracing back to their wild pig ancestors, the taxonomy for the Pot-Bellied Pig breed is *Sus scrofa.*

About 5400 years ago the Chinese issued the first book on pot-bellied pig culture.

Pot-Bellied Pigs were rediscovered about 1951 and at that time introduced into Europe as exotic zoo exhibits. They were found in Southeast Asian villages, living by night in the bamboo huts of the villagers and foraging in the daylight for food. The pigs came into the huts at night of their own free choice for warmth and out of a social need for companionship. They thereby established a basic domestic tendency.

Pigs in China/Asia have been reared and treated as members of the family. The family's pigs may be fed from the table at mealtime. They may sleep in the home and may serve as pets for the children.

Pigs have been associated with deities in many cultures. In Asia pigs are particularly highly regarded. According to legend, the Emperor Huang-Ti invented the Chinese calendar in 2637 B.C. He based it on the moon, beginning each year at the second new moon after the start of winter. He assigned an animal name to each year, one being the pig. The year of the pig (every twelve years) represents prosperity. The origin of the piggy bank in American society may be traceable back to the association of the pig with prosperity in the historic relationship between mankind and "swinekind."

Miniature pigs are becoming America's fastest growing pet animal. Each year there is a 23% growth in the number of pig lovers.

Mini pigs get along well with all animals, including horses, dogs, cats, ferrets, and people.

ARRIVAL

KEITH CONNELL IS GENERALLY RECOGNIZED AS THE FOUNDING FATHER OF THE CURRENT MINIATURE PET PIG TREND. MR. CONNELL, A ZOO DIRECTOR

THE ARRIVAL OF POT-BELLIED PIGS AS PETS

in Canada, reportedly saw the Pot-Bellied Pigs on exhibit in Europe and in 1985 imported twenty into Canada. Two of the twenty died in travel or in quarantine, leaving eighteen. Those eighteen pigs, all unrelated, became the founding breeding stock. Under Canadian law, Mr. Connell was not permitted to sell any of the original eighteen pigs imported into the country. Only the offspring could be sold or exported from Canada, and from Mr. Connell's original stock come most of the pure Pot-Bellies recognized today. Reportedly, all of the original "Connell Line" stock were black pigs.

Every new pet arrival should be 'introduced' to all the other animal members of the household. Porky meets the ferret.

There are only two lines recognized as *original* lines in the United States. Keith Leavitt, from Texas, was responsible for the second recognized line in the United States. The "Lea Line" pig has a somewhat longer nose than the "Connell Line" pig. This Leavitt Line, based in Cypress, Texas, descends from certain Pot-Bellies imported to the United States from Europe in 1989.

Although the Pot-Belly originated in the Orient, they are not numerous there today and can no longer be imported from there. The United States has forbidden any further importation, and the only pet Pot-Belly that can be registered must have lineage traceable to the breed's original stock in Canada or the United States.

Today there are more Pot-Bellied Pigs in the United States than anywhere else in the world. Their U.S. population, according to estimate, may be as high as thirty-six thousand. Since the first of these miniature pig pets arrived in North America in 1985, their popularity has exploded so swiftly that in 1990 *Vogue* magazine's Pet of the Month was the Pot-Bellied Pig.

Kayla Mull, a microbiologist and entrepreneur in Norco, California is generally credited with being the first person in the United States to actively market

There are more Pot-Bellied Pigs in the United States of America than anywhere else in the world.

ARRIVAL

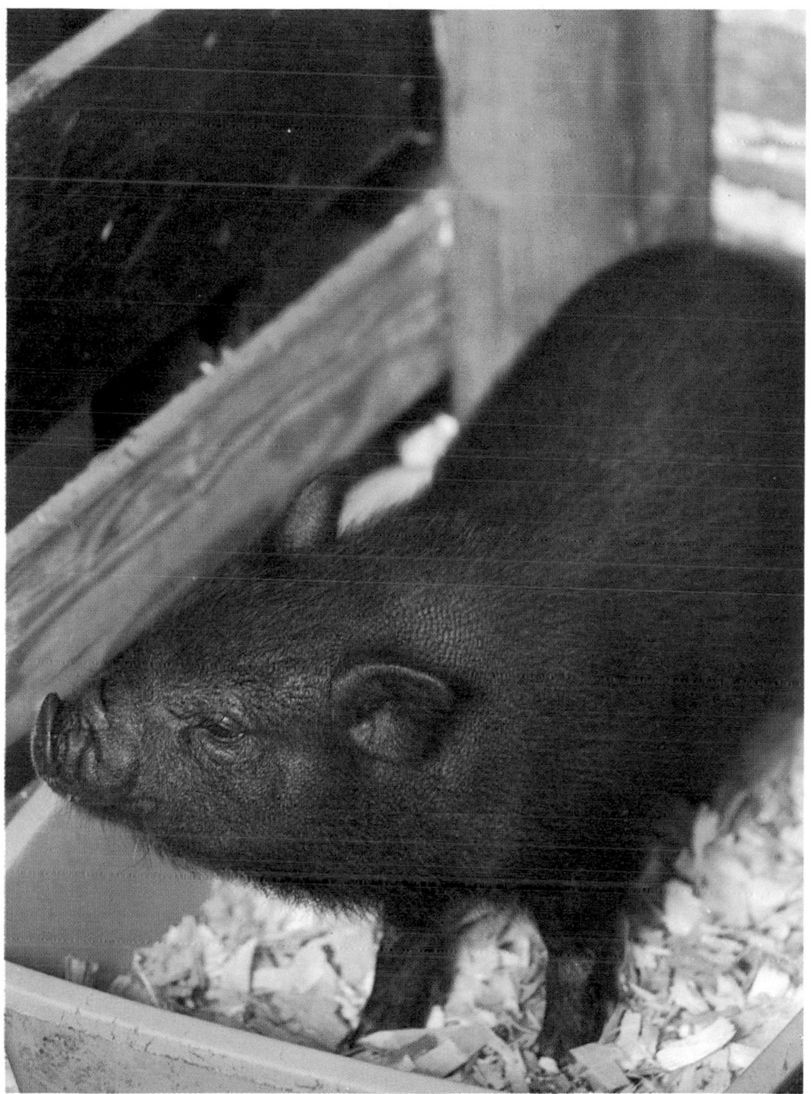

Mini pigs came to America in 1985 and within 5 years reached 32,000 in number (not counting counterfeits).

the Pot-Bellies as pets. Her company is called Creatures of Comfort.

Prices can vary quite widely for this trendiest of new "upscale" pets and depend on various factors such as current supply and anticipated demand. Indeed, the demand has been so high that breeders have been hard-pressed to meet the demand for the true, pure registered Pot-Belly. Demand for this pricey pet has been so high that people are very willing to "buy a pig in a poke," as the old expression says. Betty Scott is a breeder of Vietnamese Pot-Bellies who lives in an idyllic

The author is here providing security to a Pot-Belly by supporting it against her body with both hands.

Just like dogs, mini pigs get along with other mini pigs. Pigs are excellent pets, otherwise they wouldn't be so popular.

Pigs don't run as much as other animals, but they have a nice, steady gait.

valley near Prescott, Arizona. She explained to the author her own surprise at how eager out-of-state buyers will send her a certified check for $3000 *voluntarily,* without ever meeting her or the prospective pet piglet. She ships pet piggies all over the United States on this standard payment-in-advance basis, using a contract.

One bred Pot-Belly sow reportedly sold for $34,000. In addition to driving up the price on legitimate, registered Pot-Bellies, the pet pig craze has had other noticeable effects. Some swinophiles have taken full-sized pigs, such as Durocs, for house pets. Another effect has been the springing up, practically overnight, of a multitude of "backyard breeders." Many of them, unfortunately, are

A pedigreed Pot-Belly sow was recently sold for $34,000. Good specimens trade hands every day for $5,000.

It's not how much you pay for a mini pig that counts, as most pigs make excellent pets, but you do want the pig to stay small and that is why the pedigree is so important.

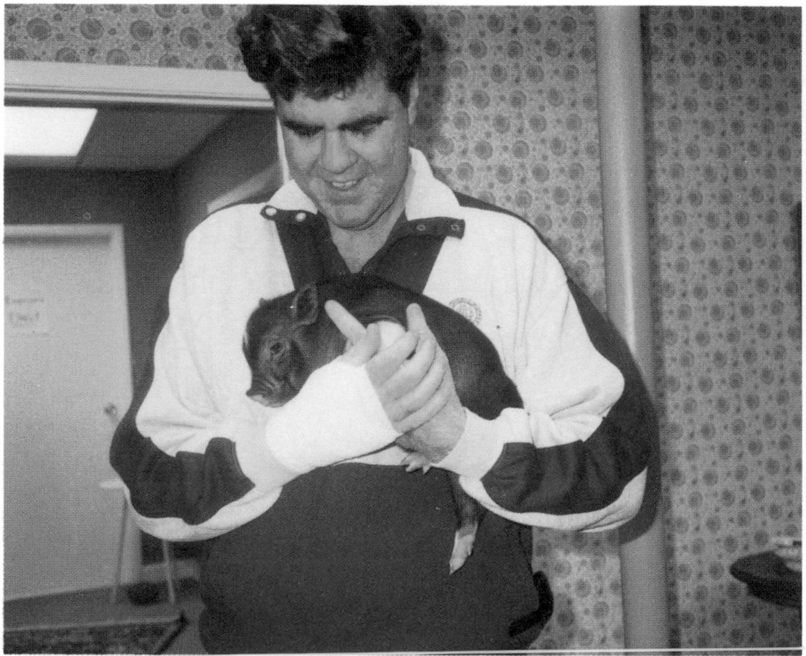

There is nothing wrong with adopting a pig which will be a few hundred pounds when it matures...as long as you know it before you buy it.

interested in cashing in on the pet pig craze, not in the ultimate health and safety of the pigs. Typically, they offer reduced prices on crossbred or other "miniatures" that may not be registered, or may not even be Pot-Bellies. If you are a true lover of animals, you can take one of these less pricey piggies home and love it just as much as you would one of his pricey cousins. However, you should do so without being fooled or misled as to what kind of pet pig you really are acquiring.

With the advent of the

growing pet pig craze, you will find fellow swine aficionados, who range from Hollywood celebrities to your next-door neighbor. If you do decide to share your home with a pet pig, too, you will be in good company. Since 1985, when the offspring of Connell's original eighteen pigs began making their way into this country to zoos and private buyers, the mini Vietnamese Pot-Bellied Pig (sometimes called Asian or Shar-Pei, as well as Chinese) population continues to grow daily!

Unless you are familiar with Pot-Bellied Pigs, you may be unable to distinguish between a baby that will grow to a few hundred pounds and a mini pig.

Above: **If the pig is secure in your grip, it will neither squirm nor squeal.**

Facing page: **Mini pigs are easy to counterfeit. If you aren't sure of your source, pay a veterinarian to pass judgment.**

COUNTERFEIT PIGS

JUST AS WITH DESIGNER JEANS, DESIGNER FRAGRANCES, AND DESIGNER HANDBAGS, THE MARKET FOR MINIATURE PIGS HAS CREATED AN unfortunate rash of "counterfeit" breeders. Usually they are backyard breeders, who set up shop overnight trying to cash in on the demand for pet pigs.

When you go to select your pet pig, there are some pitfalls to avoid. First, just because an advertisement offers miniature pigs for sale does not mean that they are miniatures. If you are attracted by a low price that looks too good to be true, it probably is. You need to be very careful in selecting your piglet.

Look for clues that the piglet may not be a genuine or purebred Pot-Belly. If the piglet has a curly tail instead of a straight one, has no sway back, or has an unusual coloration, be suspicious.

Who hasn't heard of pigtails...well, this is a mini pig's tail. If the tail is curled, it is NOT a purebred Pot-bellied Pig.

COUNTERFEIT PIGS

Pigs are available in all sizes. What you should care about is how large they will be when matured. Some can weigh a ton!

Some barnyard varieties of the standard farm pig, known as *Sus scrofa,* will reach as much as one thousand to two thousand pounds.

Besides looking at the piglets, you should ask the breeder to let you see the parents, or at least pictures of the parents if the parent pigs are not available to be seen. You also might consider asking for references of others who have purchased piglets from the breeder in the past. If the breeder is reputable, he should not object to any of your questions.

The authenticity of the registration papers is likewise subject to the principle of *caveat emptor*, or buyer beware. There have been instances of forged or altered registration papers. In order to be sure of the veracity of any registration papers, call the registry and verify the registration information directly. Be certain, as well, that the registration papers fit the piglet. If the registry verifies that the papers you are holding are genuine, that does not guarantee that the piglet is. If the piglet has a curly tail and hair that parts down the middle of his back, he is part domestic farm pig, and the "authentic" registration papers that accompanied him will not make him grow up to be the purebred mini Pot-Belly you expected when you bought him.

Further assurance that you will not be selecting the wrong piglet for your pet means studying the

You don't need a doggy bed for your pet mini pig. When he's tired, any place will do.

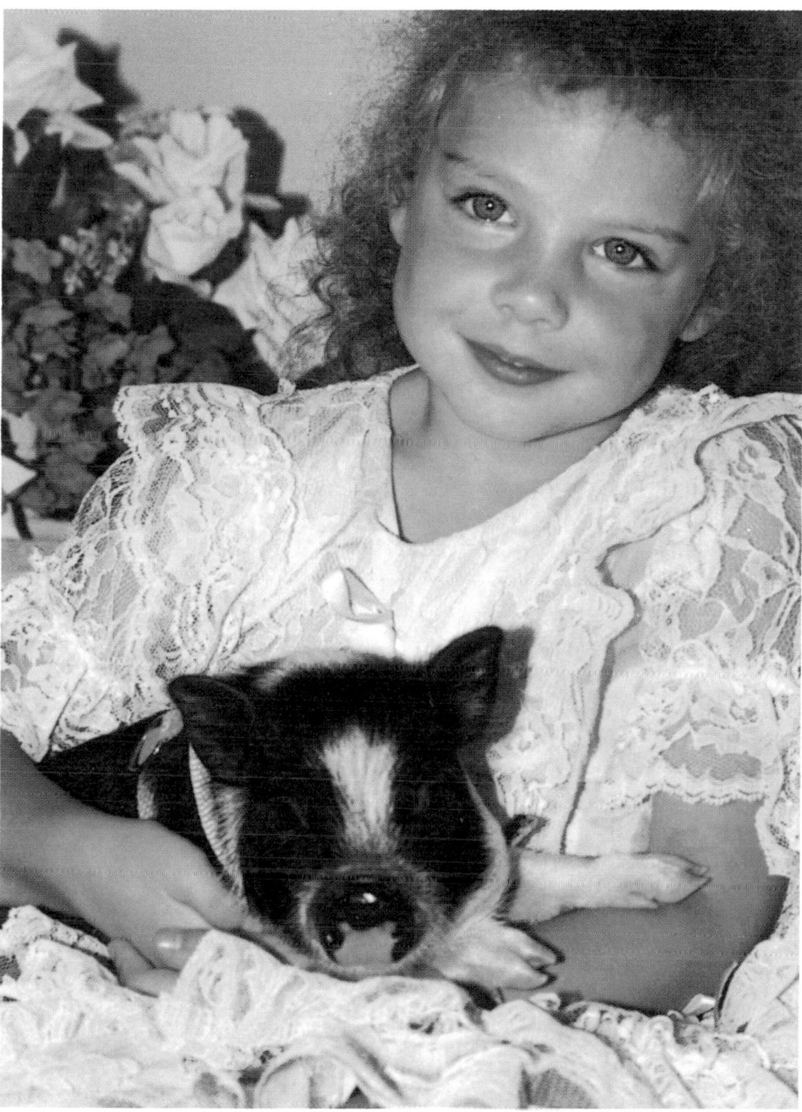

If you have any doubt about the pig's being a mini, don't buy it. Try to obtain a guarantee as to the maximum size to which the pig will grow. Tattoos make identification more positive.

standards. When you see the sire and dam—or pictures of them—look for poor conformation as well as for size. Poor conformation can be seen in knocked knees, bony hips, a straight forehead, or a snout that is too long.

When selecting your pet piglet, you also should expect a health certificate and the right to an examination by your own vet. The veterinarian's examination, which normally would be at your cost, is probably the best means to obtain an expert assurance that the piglet is not a "counterfeit," is of the correct conformation, and is healthy.

Large, protective dogs like Rottweilers should be carefully introduced to your mini pig or the natural reaction of the dog might result in the destruction of the mini pig.

Isn't this the face only a mother can love? A good mini has a short snout, wrinkles, and a short forehead.

BREED DESCRIPTION

Pot-Bellied Pigs live longer than dogs. Some live for 30 years.

THE VIETNAMESE POT-BELLIES CAN BE LONG-LIVED, GIVEN THE PROPER DIET, EXERCISE, AND HEALTH CARE. SOME ESTIMATE THE LIFESPAN TO be fifteen to twenty-five years. Others estimate eighteen to thirty years. Since these diminutive porkers are such newcomers as pets, we will need for at least the first generation or so to live out their natural lifespans as house pets in order to determine which of the longevity estimates is more accurate.

Even as the mini pigs mature, their weights vary. True-bred Pot-Bellied Pigs can weigh from 35 to 150 pounds when mature.

SIZE

The average Pot-Belly will continue to grow for about two years. Full-grown mini pigs that have been adequately fed can range in weight from about thirty-five to one hundred and fifty pounds. Height at the shoulder will range generally from ten to twenty inches. Please note that these general ranges applicable to the full spectrum of the breed will exceed the more restrictive ranges established as "standards" by the North American Potbelly Pig Association (NAPPA).

Even large mini pigs don't grow tall. A 150-pound pig will be less than two feet tall. Dogs are larger but lighter in weight.

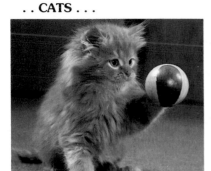

"Stop eating like a pig!" You can train a pig to do lots of things, but you can't train him to eat properly.

COLORATION

The miniature Pot-Belly is predominantly black, including the skin, hair, and hooves. White areas may be present. Where white meets black, there typically may be a region of white hair over black skin with a resultant gray appearance. Parent pigs who are entirely black may have progeny exhibiting areas of white coloration. Conversely, parent pigs with white coloring may throw offspring that are entirely black.

EYES

The eyes are deep set and black in color, or brown, usually.

Miniature Pot-bellied Pigs are usually black, but they can have offspring with patches of white. True breeding for color has not yet been established (homozygous pigs).

Mini pigs have deep-set dark, usually black, eyes.

CONFORMATION

The pure Pot-Belly will have a short, "pug" nose with a dished face. Some wrinkling is usually present. Short upright ears are present over thick rolls of jowl. The sway back may have wrinkling. The pot-belly is prominent. In fact, the females' bellies will tend to drag the ground late in gestation due to the short legs of the pig. The tail is straight, with a bushy switch of hair on the end.

Miniature pigs in general are about one-tenth the size of the average barnyard Hampshire or Duroc cousin. Female Pot-Bellies, interestingly, are larger than the males when adult. Also, the

The ideal conformation is a short pug nose, with a dished face. Short ears that stand up by themselves. It must have a belly, of course. The animal shown here is typical of Pot-Belly pigs.

The belly of female Pot-Bellied Pigs may drop so much they drag along the ground during the latter part of their pregnancy since their legs are so short.

female reportedly will continue to grow larger in size with the birth of each litter. On average, the mini pigs are about the height of your coffee table.

The pinto (black and white) coloration is generally the result of selective breeding of the black Pot-Bellies in an effort to get more of the desired white coloring in combination with the black. However, pinto also could result from the crossing of black Pot-Bellies with white Pot-Bellies.

The white Pot-Bellies, frequently called Royal White or Imperial White, are white in coloration. They may have blue eye coloration. The white Pot-Belly is not an albino, or unpigmented, Pot-Belly. It is a true color. It has the standard sway back and characteristic pot-belly. That paunch, by the way, is believed to be a genetic trait that is a biological holdover from the generations of ancestors eating water-soaked pond lilies in ancient China.

SWEDISH MINIATURE WHITES

Swedish Miniature Whites generally are not considered to be Pot-Bellies, although it seems that unanimity has not been achieved on this question. The registry in Indiana, which accepts only Pot-Bellies, does not accept for registration the

During the course of pregnancy, the female Pot-Belly pigs, heavy with fat and babies, may require being penned up with a deep hay bottom to protect their undersides.

Regular farm animals are identified with ear clips. The floppy ears and the curly tail (not visible in this photo) indicate this is NOT a miniature animal.

Swedish Whites, or any other non-Pot-Belly miniature pigs. The Swedish Miniature Whites are registered with the American Miniature Pig Association in Douglasvllle, Georgia and with the International Gold Star Potbelly Pig Registry in Pescadero, California.

These Swedish Whites resulted from the wish of John P. Bailey—Global Exotics, Inc.—to import a line of pigs based on specific standards for quality and conformation. Mr. Bailey researched pigs in Scandinavia and England before deciding to import the Swedish Miniature Whites. These he found to have been bred down for size and color.

Global Exotics, Inc. was formed to import the Swedish Whites. In March, 1990 Roger Cresswell was sent to Sweden to pick the foundation stock for Global Exotics. This line was imported directly

There are other miniature pigs, like the Swedish White, which is smaller than the Vietnamese Pot-Belly. But the Pot-Belly (shown below) has more fanciers than the Swedish White.

Pot-Belly clubs are in! Of course they are talking about pigs and not fat old men!

from Sweden into the United States.

Mr. Bailey, a Florida entrepreneur, has documentation that his founding stock are Swedish born, specifically bred for size and color, and are of a line of pigs that were originally purchased from the European zoo system. The ancestors of these Swedish Whites apparently originated in Southeast Asia, but they had been bred in Sweden for a good number of years. (The pigs are properly approved by the United States Department of Agriculture and the

There are many types of miniature pigs other than the Pot-Belly. Many of these pigs have been crossed with the Pot-Belly. Think about cross-bred dogs and you have the picture with pigs.

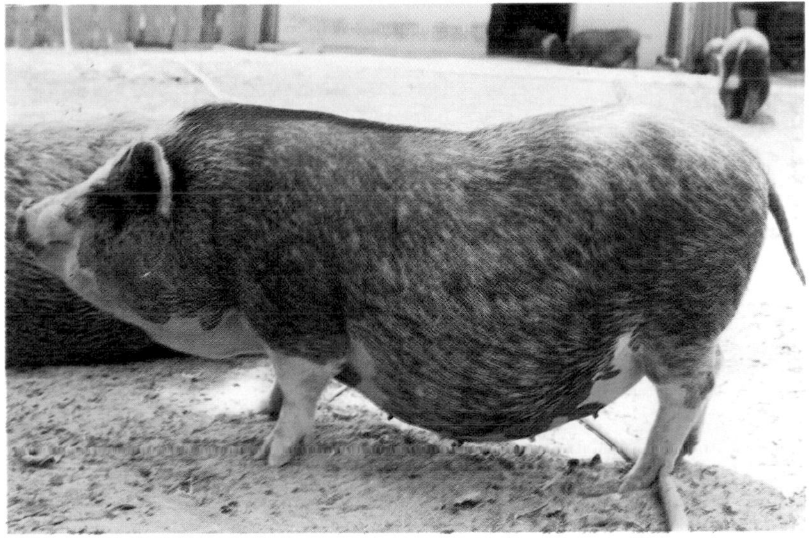

A Pot-Belly requires almost the same care as most other miniature pigs, but its short legs and heavy belly do require special attention.

Swedish Ministry of Agriculture.)

These mini Swedish Whites generally are under twelve inches in height. The weight is from twenty to forty pounds when full grown. The standards set for the White Line foundation stock were: traceable lineage, small size, straight tail, and short nose.

OTHER TYPES OF MINIATURE PIGS

Other types of miniature pet pigs that are not Pot-Bellies include: African Juliani, Juliani Pot-Bellies (a cross of the Juliani with the Pot-Belly), Hormel Sinclair, Micro, Colony, and African Guinea or Pygmy Pigs.

Specific information on each type can be

obtained from the breeders who offer that given mini pig type for sale. In general, the information on nutrition, care, training, and so forth given in this book for Pot-Bellies can be applied for your pet mini pig, regardless of his type.

Scott Ranch in Prescott, Arizona breeds the rare Juliani pigs. Coloration may be silver, white, black, red, black and white, or black and red.

Ossabaw Island Pigs, registered with the American Minor Breeds Conservancy (A.M.B.C.),

Though it is difficult to prove, Pot-Belly pigs from Vietnam are the best as pets.

Any pig can be made into a pet animal if you give it the time, love and devotion necessary. But it would be a shame if the animal grew so large that it could not be kept in your home.

range from forty to one hundred and twenty-five pounds. Their coloration may be red, black, white (not common), red/black/white spotted, red/black spotted, or black/white spotted.

One lesser known type, referred to as the "Viking Pig," reportedly is a cross or hybrid that originated out of Scotland.

PIG REGISTRY

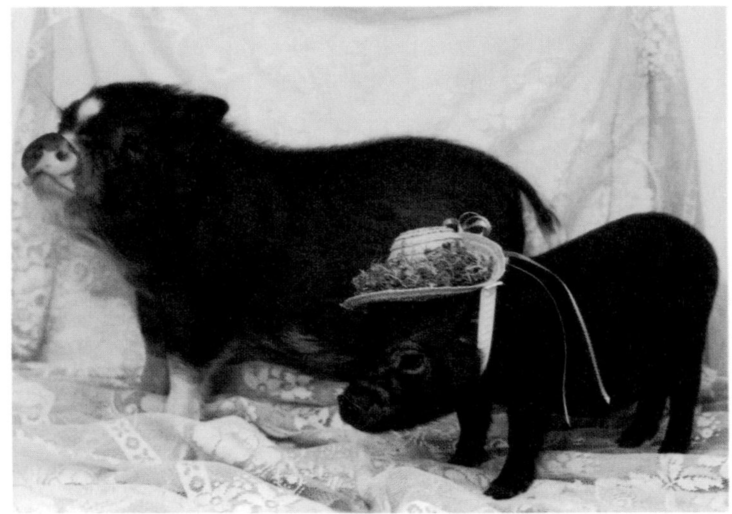

Brother and sister. Not all pigs grow to the same size.

THE INTERNATIONAL GOLD STAR REGISTRY SERVICE WAS FOUNDED IN JUNE, 1988 BY KIYOKO HANCOCK. IT REPORTEDLY IS THE ORIGINAL INTERNATIONAL

POT-BELLIED PIG REGISTRY SERVICES

registry for miniature pigs. All pigs registered with this registry must be purebreds, with lineage traceable to the original Connell Line in Canada or to the Leavitt Line. Purebreds with lineage traceable to three other specific lines are also acceptable: the Lone Star Line of Texas; Global Exotics Imperial; FWF Majestic Line.

This registry's stated purpose is to develop a standard of excellence for the breed; to help develop conscientious breeding programs; to protect and promote the Pot-Belly Pig; and to educate and support pig owners. The Gold Star Service has "closed" stud books, which insures the integrity of the registry and provides the complete lineage on the pig. Having the complete pedigree allows the owner to know if any crossbreeding or improper breeding has occurred.

Also, the Gold Star Registry has specifically promoted the Pot-Belly as a "mental health worker" in animal-assisted therapy programs. As little ambassadors for the breed, Pot-Bellies are taken to rehabilitation centers, convalescent homes, pediatric hospitals, and psychiatric care units throughout the United States. The gentle little porkers have proven to be well suited for this community service work.

The Gold Star Registry endorses and supports the efforts of the North American Potbelly Pig Association (NAPPA). Pigs registered with the

Mini pigs eat everything...and they are especially fond of human treats, as this youngster learned the hard way!

Gold Star Registry are qualified to be shown in any NAPPA-sanctioned event, if they are registered in the Gold Star Division.

The International Gold Star Registry has a White Star Research Division, as well as the Gold Star Division. The white pigs registered in the White Star Division do not meet NAPPA standards and cannot be shown at NAPPA-sponsored or sanctioned events. In September 1990 the White Star Research Division opened a new stud book to track and record the White Pot-Belly Pig in the U.S. The intent of this effort was the observation, research, and study of these white miniature pigs with the help and guidance of geneticists, nutritionists, breeders, and veterinarians.

To qualify for Gold Star Division registration, your pet piggy must have birth certificates or equivalent documentation of lineage traceable to the original Connell Canadian group of pigs or to the United States importation from Europe via the Lea Line and/or Global Exotics Imperial Line, Lone Star Line of Texas, or FWF Majestic Line. The address for the International Gold Star Registry is P.O. Box 227, Pescadero, California 94060.

THE POT-BELLIED PIG REGISTRATION SERVICE

This Indiana-based registry is owned by Betty Beeman and her husband Dale. It was started in the fall of 1988 as a means of keeping track of the Pot-Bellied piggies and their lineage. It began with fifty charter members. Today, it is the largest registry service for Pot-Bellies in the world. As of March 1991, the official count of this registry reportedly was twenty-five thousand (25,000) documented, registered Pot-Bellies,

If you want to locate a source for a mini pig, contact any of the names and addresses mentioned in this book.

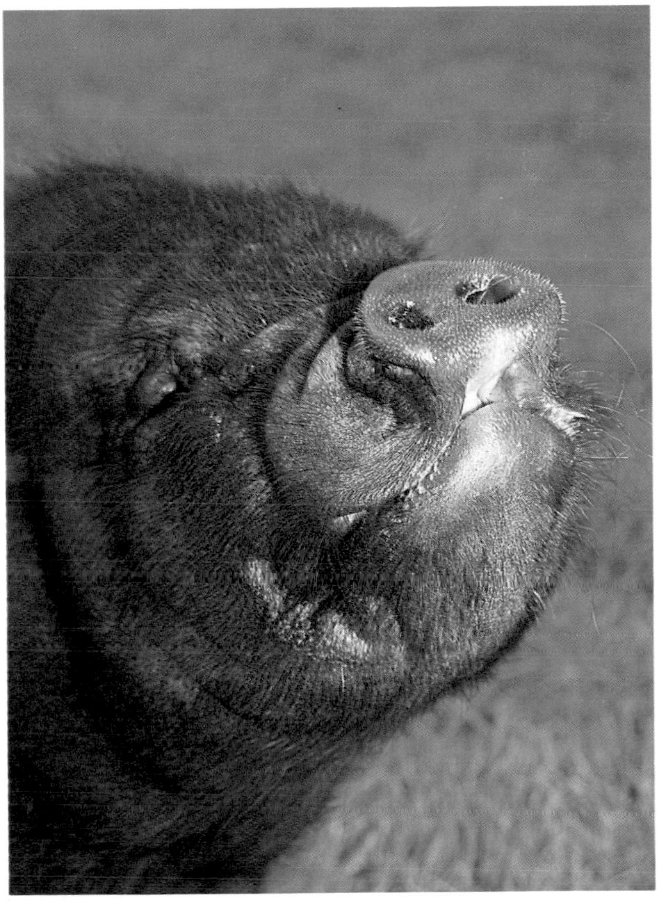

and the number is growing daily.

This registry has accepted only Pot-Bellies, which does include the Royal Whites. It has not accepted any other miniature pigs to date, including the Swedish White, the Juliani, or others. The address is 22819 Stanton Road, Lakeville, Indiana 46536.

This service, which began as a husband and wife "cottage industry" business, now reportedly employs eight full-time employees, some part-time help, and utilizes several computers in expanding office facilities to record and track the burgeoning number of pet Pot-Bellies. This growing enterprise also works closely with NAPPA to help promote the pigs and pig-related events, such as shows and seminars. It also publishes a newsletter.

AMERICAN MINIATURE PIG ASSOCIATION

This registry service is located in Douglasville, Georgia. It is smaller than the two principal registry services. The American Miniature Pig Association does accept the Swedish White Miniature for registrations, as well as the Juliani pig. This organization's address is P.O. Box 116, Douglasville, Georgia 30133.

A merger of the American Miniature Pig Association and the Pot-Bellied Pig Registration Service is reportedly in the planning stages.

STANDARD

According to NAPPA, the maximum weight of a Pot-Belly is 95 pounds, but the ideal weight is about 50 pounds.

THE NORTH AMERICAN POTBELLY PIG ASSOCIATION (NAPPA) ESTABLISHED A RECOMMENDED STANDARD FOR AMERICAN POT-BELLIED PIGS AT ITS BOARD MEETING ON FEBRUARY 10, 1990.

STANDARD FOR THE AMERICAN POT-BELLIED PIG

That standard is as follows:

General Appearance: Structurally symmetrical. Free of obvious defects. Short legs. Smooth flowing lines. Pronounced pot-belly. Swayed back. Erect ears. Straight tail.

Weight: Maximum acceptable weight of ninety-five pounds. Ideal weight being less than fifty pounds.

Height: Maximum acceptable height of eighteen inches. Ideal height being less than fourteen inches. To be measured at the withers, high point of the shoulders, with legs being straight underneath.

The maximum height for a Pot-Belly is 18 inches, but 14 inches is more desirable.

Length: In acceptable proportion to height.

Skin: Color should be black, or black and white. Hair should lay evenly over the back, with seasonal variation. Wrinkles may or may not be present.

Head: Ears should be small and erect, and somewhat flat. Nose should be short to medium length, in proportion to the head, allowing for free passage of air when breathing normally. Eyes should be deep and wide-set, clear, and of varying color, except red being evident of albinism. Jowl should be obvious and in proportion to the head. Bite should be even and correct, and should not be either overshot or undershot.

The ideal Pot-Belly is black or black and white.

Body: Back should be swayed through the saddle. Shoulder should be sloping evenly from side to side. Neck should be short. Rump should flow gently to the base of the tail. Tail should be straight and of medium length, with a switch on the end. Belly, viewed from the side, should be rounded obviously, but not exaggerated or touching the ground. Viewed from the top, the belly should not round from the backbone and have only a slight lateral protuberance. Teats should be at least five pairs, evenly spaced.

Feet and Legs: Legs should be wide-set standing well on the pasterns. Feet, standing squarely, should have two toes of equal length on each foot pointing forward.

Disposition: Should be tractable (docile; easily controlled) and non-aggressive.

All measurements in the standard are based on pigs one year of age.

Before you buy your Pot-Belly, study all of those offered to you. Handle them. Talk to them. Find the one with a personality compatible with your own.

HOME

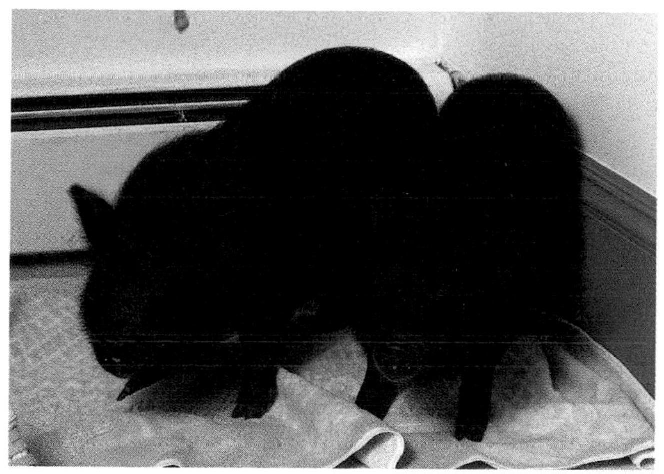

When you first bring your pet pig home, expect it to be shy and frightened. Give it a chance to acclimate itself to its new surroundings.

TO MAKE YOUR NEW PET'S ADJUSTMENT TO HIS NEW HOME WITH YOU AS SMOOTH AS POSSIBLE, YOU SHOULD HAVE EVERYTHING PREPARED IN ADVANCE FOR

BRINGING HOME THE BACON

his arrival. Whether you are picking him up or having him delivered, his home should be ready for him. This means having his food, his food and water bowls (heavy crock-type bowls that he cannot tip over are recommended), his litter box, and his bed waiting for him. The bed may be a large dog cage or crate with bedding that the piglet can burrow in when he sleeps. Soft old comforters are ideal.

If your piglet has not been handled much, be prepared for the fact that he is going to squirm and squeal in fear the first time you pick him up. It is most important that you handle him properly, or he might wriggle free and fall to the floor, injuring himself. Never pick the piglet up by his legs. Pick him up in a gentle cradling hold such that his weight is balanced. Hold him against you gently but firmly so that he does not wriggle free.

The piglet will squeal when you first pick him up. Do not respond to the squealing by putting the piglet back down, if possible. Doing that will begin to condition the piglet to believe that he can always get put back down if he squeals hard enough. That is not a learned response you will want him to have. Instead, when he squeals, cup your hand gently over his snout to quiet him. This gives him a feeling of security. Eventually, he will be trusting and quiet when you pick him up if you let him know that he is secure and is not going to

Your new piglet will probably squeal and wriggle when it is first picked up. Be prepared...don't drop the piglet.

fall or be hurt. You should not let any small children pick up the piglet until you are sure that they have learned how to handle him properly.

Adhering to the following precautions can help to ensure the safety of your pet:

•Do not keep the piglet's bed or "house" near cold drafts. Also, it should not be near the television. High frequencies that are inaudible for humans may be painful for animals.

Make your home safe from any hazards to the piglet. Common hazards include:

•Medications—Remember that pigs will eat just about anything that they can get into.

•Swimming pools—Although pigs are excellent swimmers, they can drown easily if left unattended and are unable to climb out.

•Poisonous house plants—These should be removed from your pet's living quarters.

•Paint fumes—Your pet should never be exposed to the fumes of paint or any other similar substance.

•Cleaning fluids and all other potentially harmful liquids and chemicals—Keep materials such as these in a secure place away from your pet.

•Neighborhood dogs—To a tiny "swinelet," dogs are predators. Your piglet can be killed or badly injured.

•Theft or escape—Pig pilfering, sadly, does occur. If you let your pig outside, be sure you have a strong fence that he cannot root under and that thieves cannot enter through.

When you first bring home your baby piglet, keep it in a confined area at first. A single room,

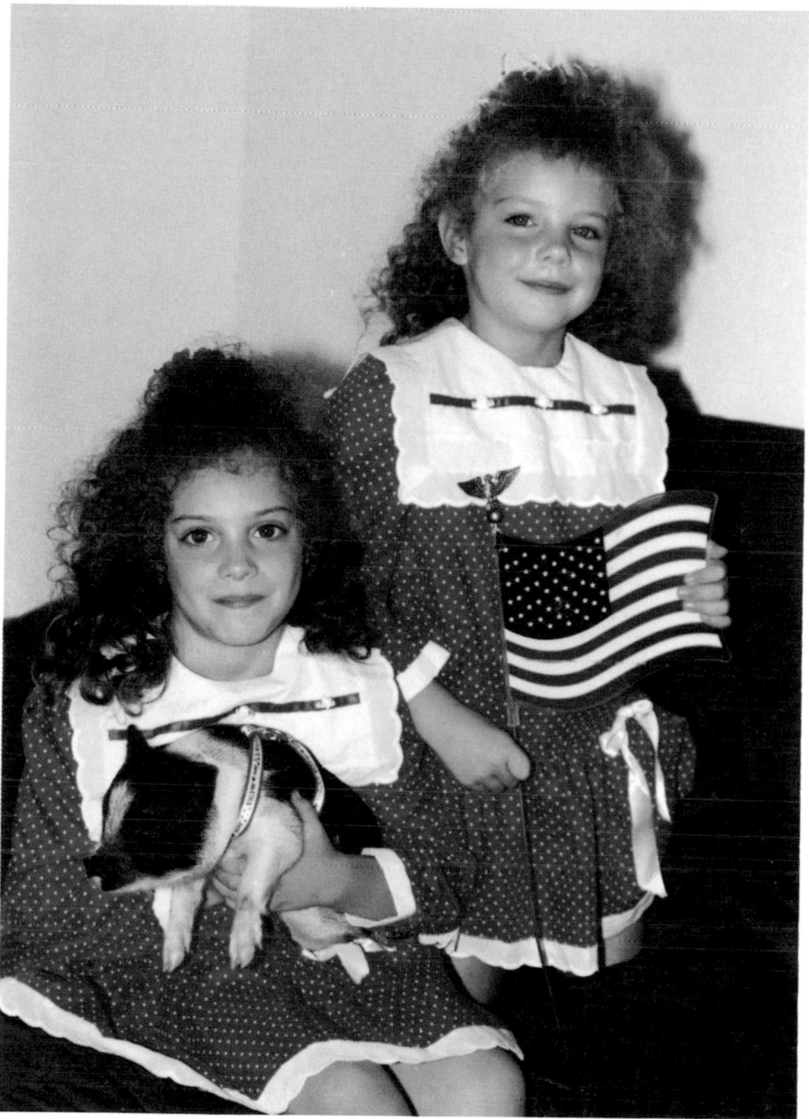

There is a new breed of pig called the "American Pot-Bellied Pig." It is bred to different standards than most mini pigs.

such as the kitchen, that you spend a lot of time in is best. This lets you socialize more with him initially. Your presence will be comforting to him and will reduce the stress of his adjustment to his new surroundings. Spend as much time as possible with him during the first week. Let him adjust to your home gradually, one room at a time. Talk to him reassuringly as much as possible. Be sure that he knows where his litter box is (if you use the litter box method for housebreaking, as opposed to taking your piggie outside). Usually, the pet pig is kept primarily inside the house, and either taken out on walks and for exercise or allowed access to a yard area. If you want to allow him free access, the commercial pet doors work very well.

If you have other pets at your home, introduce the new piglet to them slowly. Praise each pet equally to avoid jealousy and insecurity. Adjustment will take a few days. Do not leave the pets alone together unattended until after you have made sure they are thoroughly adjusted to each other. Another important factor in avoiding potential conflict is making sure that you never feed the animals together. Your piglet should have his own "dining area," with his own food and bowls, separate from any other pet's. Also, please show proper consideration for

***Facing Page:* It is preferable to handle the new piglet when you are on the ground in case it jumps or wriggles free. Don't worry about the squealing. Just cup his snout gently with your hand.**

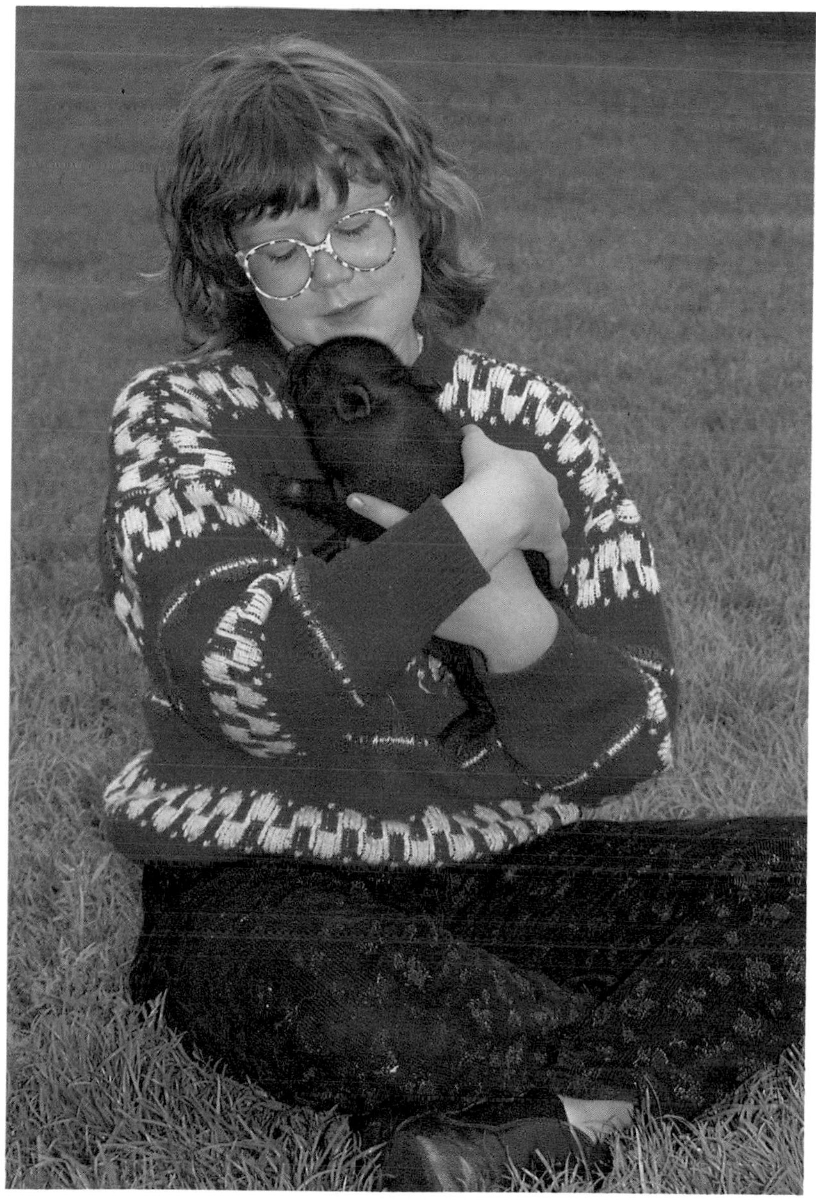

your pet by not putting his feeding area next to his litter box.

For night sleeping you can cover your pig's crate with a blanket or other cover, just as you would cover a bird's cage.

If you put any kind of collar or harness on your piglet, it should be loose enough for comfort. It should be made of cotton webbing or other soft material that will not irritate his skin. Also, do not leave any such things on your pig when you leave him home alone, as he could get caught on something and injure himself.

You know you have won your piglet over when he comes to you of his own free will and signals you to pick him up.

Fresh water should be available for your pig at all times.

For cooling your piglet in the summer heat, you should provide a source of water for soaking and cooling. A child's shallow plastic swimming pool works very nicely. Or, you can keep a hose available for hosing the piglet down to cool him.

Finally, when bringing home your baby porker, please recognize that even though you become his "owner," you really cannot "own" him. (Nor should you want to.) You can only live with him, share your home with him, and make him a part of your family.

If you intend to take your pig for a walk, get a suitable harness.

The harness for a mini pig should be loose, wide webbed, and made from a soft material which will not irritate its skin.

FEEDING

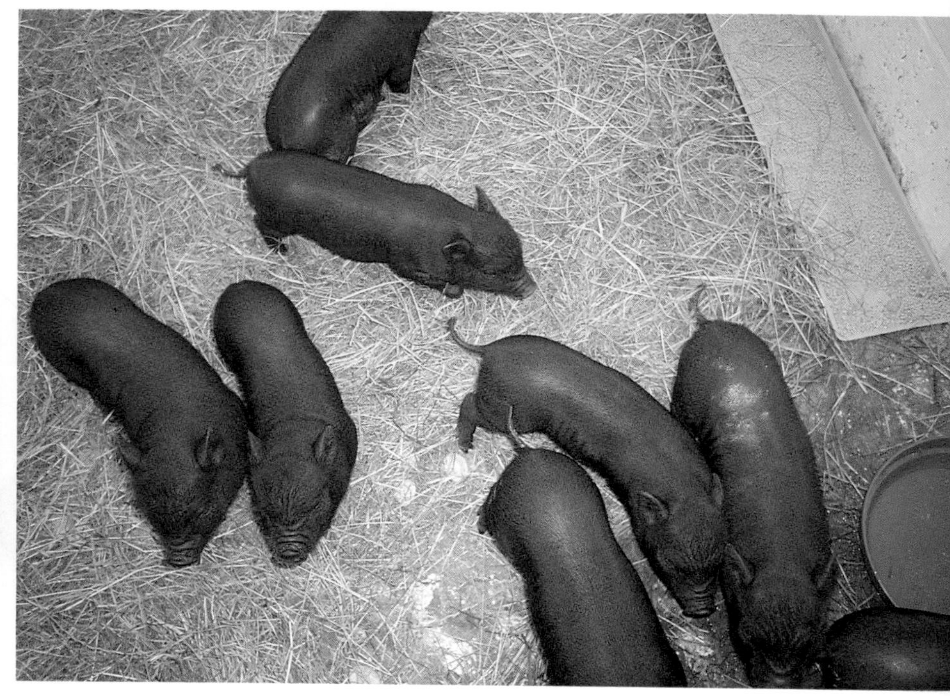

TECHNICALLY, YOUR PORCINE COMPANION IS AN OMNIVORE. THAT MEANS THAT IN THE WILD THE POT-BELLY WILL EAT MEAT (LIKE

Facing page: **Pigs are always eating. The more they eat, the bigger they become.**

Above: **Pigs eat just about everything, including many things which are poisonous. Supervise their feed.**

FEEDING AND NUTRITION

a carnivore) as well as vegetables and fruits (like a herbivore). In the home, your Pot-Belly is equally omnivorous. He will eat just about *anything* in any of the four food groups, in other words!!! He, however, should not be permitted to eat indiscriminately. Overeating and incorrect eating can both be dangerous to your piggy's health, and it is up to you his owner to make sure that he does not endanger himself by indulging himself in uncontrolled and unmonitored eating. You need to be aware that your pig has no self-control in the eating department. Left to his own devices, he *will* literally "pig out."

Grapes may be your pig's most favorite food.

It is important to recognize that you cannot feed regular swine food, which was developed for livestock, to your pet pig. The commercial swine foods have a content that is intended only to fatten pigs and to be fed over the relatively short lifespan of a feeder pig. It lacks the nutrients

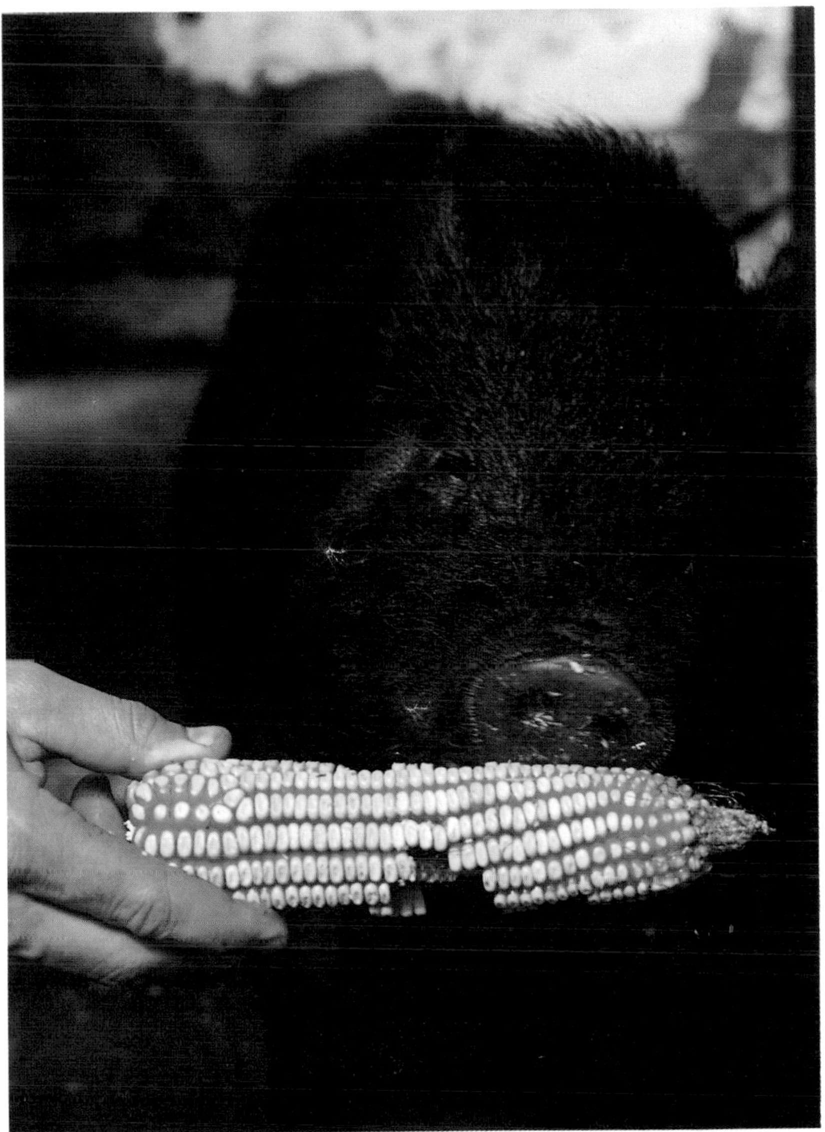

Corn is NOT recommended for your mini pig. Popcorn is, however, fine—as a treat.

necessary to maintain a healthy pet animal.

Foods specially formulated for miniature pigs are available from most feed dealers. For example, Purina offers a line of miniature pet pig food that is designed to meet the nutritional needs of your pet from "piglethood" to adulthood.

As the popularity of these little porkers continues to grow, it is only a matter of time before this specialized food will be available at pet shops.

In addition, your pig should receive some other "munchies" each day to provide roughage and variety for him. "This little piggy ate roast beef" is part of a very familiar old rhyme, but roast beef and other meats (including roast pork) are not recommended for the Pot-Bellies. Meats are too high in protein. Your pet porker will readily ingest most any table scraps, but such a diet is not advisable either.

Feed your pig from a pot, don't cast the food on the floor.

Facing page: **Pet shops that handle exotic animals like goats, sheep, and pigs have specialty foods for mini pigs.**

FEEDING

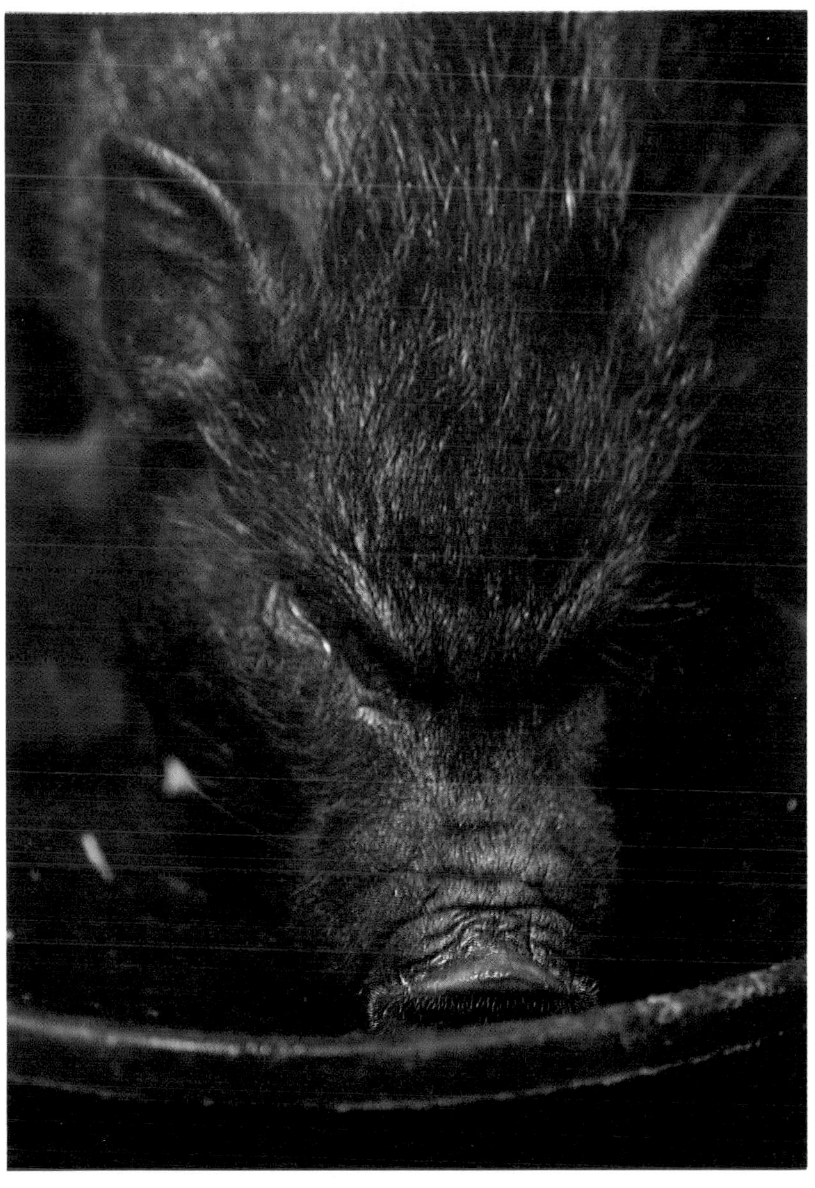

Rather, the recommended source for your piggy's needed roughage is various fruits and vegetables, or a "salad" of mixed ingredients.

One fruit that is highly recommended is papaya. It is high in Vitamin C and minerals. Also, the black seeds in papaya seem to act as a natural wormer for the pig. The papain present in papaya will act as a deodorizer to freshen your piggy's breath and reduce odor from his waste. Sarsaponin, a sarsaparilla root extract, also apparently acts as a biological odor remover for control of the ammonia odor in pig waste.

Avocados and banana leaves are good for the skin condition. In addition, you can treat your pig with tiny bits of apples, peas, bananas, lettuce, grapes, and other fruits and vegetables during the day.

For his basic daily diet regimen, it is most important to keep your pig on high quality feed that is especially formulated for mini pigs. This is the only way to insure that he receives all the essential vitamins and minerals for his nutritional requirements. If you try to use an alternative food, because it is cheaper, or a dog food (because it is easier to get), you will only be doing your little friend and family member a disservice.

For your porky pal to remain small and healthy, you will have to monitor his diet closely. Your veterinarian can give you a suggested feeding guide. The quantity of food will be adjusted depending on such

If your mini pig gets into your garden, he will probably destroy all the newly sprouting plants, trample everything, and perhaps become ill from the herbicide and fertilizer. Keep your pig under control.

factors as size, age, climate (more food is needed in colder winter months than in summer, for example), level of activity, and exercise.

In planning your pet's diet, take these recommended factors into consideration:

good taste, low food intake to accomplish full nutrition needs, high digestibility, and promotion of healthy skin and hair.

Consult your veterinarian with any

questions, and be certain that your vet understands Pot-Bellied Pigs in particular, as well as general pet needs.

Perhaps the most critical factor in your porcine pet's diet is water. *Clean, fresh water.* Keep it available at all times. A spill-proof, heavy crock is best so that the pig cannot tip it over or slosh the water out by rooting the bowl with his snout. A Pot-Belly can dehydrate in a matter of hours, and he should never be left without water.

Diet supplements should be considered only in consultation with your veterinarian. There are various vitamins and minerals that are particularly important to the pig and that might be needed by your individual Pot-Belly as an additional supplement to his regular diet.

Vitamin E and selenium are two dietary elements that tend to deplete and therefore may become a deficiency for your pig. Vitamin E acts as an antioxidant and is vital to proper cellular membrane maintenance and to other body functions.

Vitamin D is essential for absorption of magnesium and calcium from the small intestine. It is also important for maintenance of proper blood levels of calcium and phosphorus. The calcium and phosphorus, in turn, are vital to skeletal development and to various metabolic functions.

Vitamin A is important for your pig in the proper development and maintenance of body membranes, in vision, in reproduction, and in growth. If the pig's dietary intake and/or storage of

Vitamin A in the liver are not adequate, his overall health can deteriorate.

Choline, as part of acetylcholine, is an important element for proper function of the nervous system and for other body processes. It also is involved in the processing of fatty acids, through both oxidation and phosphorylation (the enzymatic conversion of carbohydrates in metabolic processes). Choline additionally serves as a source of methyl groups, important chemical compounds in

Not many veterinarians are knowledgeable about miniature pigs. Locate a good vet before you need one. This is especially true if you expect to breed your pig.

cellular functions.

Although this technical nutritional information is admittedly very dry and boring, it may help you and your veterinarian better plan for your pet pig's needs. If your pig is a baby when you bring him home, he will most likely have other specific needs. Baby pigs, for example, have a very limited ability to maintain energy homeostasis. Limited gluconeogenesis (formation of glucose within the body from

The dietary needs of small pigs are not much different from the needs of larger pigs, except small pigs require fatty acids. Ask your pet supplier for these supplements.

proteins, fats, and substances other than carbohydrates), together with low body fat stores, will exacerbate the effects of hypoglycemia for a young pig. A supplement may be needed to provide neonatal (newborn) and young piglets an energy source to complement the piglet's own natural lipolysis (the hydrolysis of fat) process and rate of fatty acid oxidation. It is also necessary to provide additional energy substrates (substances acted upon by an enzyme) in order to spare glucose and glycogen energy stores, which are at a premium and are rapidly depleted in young piglets.

For your baby Pot-Belly, a critical energy source for replacement of this lipid energy is fatty acids. Fatty acids, as we all certainly remember vividly from our high school chemistry class, are the "building blocks" of fat. Through the oxidation of fatty acids, a supplemental energy is generated, which is critical for a young piggy's needs.

The four fatty acids that comprise seventy to eighty percent of your mini-swine pet's natural lipid energy source are: stearic, palmitic, linoleic, and oleic.

If the dietary intake of these essential fatty acids is insufficient, overall health will suffer. If your piglet has a poor coat, or poor skin and hair condition, this may very well be indicative of deficiencies in fatty acids. Besides the skin and coat, the essential fatty acids are also important to the proper development and maintenance of various membrane systems in the pig's body. These membrane systems are vital to proper body function and as the initial barrier to disease.

However, this guide is only general. Remember that each pig is an individual and that you should adjust his diet according to his own needs.

TREATS—FOODS THAT YOUR MINI PIG WILL GO "HOG WILD" FOR

Treats can be used especially effectively in training your pig. Some that seem to be favorites with the Pot-Bellies are suggested here: watermelon rind, grapes,

Even though pigs eat everything, they still must have a balanced diet. The fatty acids (stearic, palmitic, linoleic and oleic) are all necessary.

FEEDING

cereal, salad (tomatoes and green peppers not recommended), popcorn (no salt, no butter), sliced apple, oranges, raisins, and melon.

FOODS TO AVOID

The following food items should be avoided: corn—hard to digest (popcorn is fine if it has no salt or butter), salt—in excess it can cause saline shock, and chocolate—believed to be potentially poisonous to Pot-Bellies. In addition, certain plants are known to be, or can be, poisonous. These include tar weed, St. Johnswort, buttercup, rhubarb, hemlock, any growing mushroom, lily of the valley, and others.

***Facing page:* Pigs eat like pigs...and in many cases they can be fed your table scraps like watermelon rinds, apple cores, dried grapes, melon rinds and most green vegetables like the outer leaves of lettuce.**

FEEDING

You can train your pig to 'beg' for food.

GROOMING

CONTRARY TO THEIR UNDESERVED REPUTATION, PIGS ACTUALLY ARE VERY CLEAN ANIMALS. IF THEY ARE NOT KEPT IN AN UNCLEAN PEN—AS FARM PIGS USUALLY ARE—THEY PREFER TO AND WILL KEEP THEMSELVES AS CLEAN AS POSSIBLE. FOR YOUR PET "HOUSE PIG," GROOMING REQUIREMENTS ARE RELATIVELY SIMPLE. IF YOUR PIGGY IS TO BE A

THE FASTIDIOUS PIG— GROOMING CARE FOR POT-BELLIED PIGS

healthy and happy member of the family, good pig hygiene and grooming are, just as with other pets, an essential part of preventive health care.

THE OILED PIG (NOT TO BE CONFUSED WITH THE "GREASED PIG")

Pot-Bellies tend to have dry skin. If you do not want your pet to have a skin like "pork rinds," then you must oil your pig's skin weekly. If you live in a dry climate, more frequent oilings may be necessary. You can use an unperfumed skin lotion or mineral oil. However, if your pig goes outside, sand or dirt may stick to skin oiled with these products. Another school of thought on the subject of oiling holds that the procedure shouldn't be necessary if the pig has a properly balanced diet.

BRUSHING—THE "HYPOALLERGENIC" PIG

Some Pot-Bellies love brushing; others tolerate it. The skin should be kept as clean as possible at all times, and brushing frequently is advisable. The pig has hair rather than fur. For this reason, he also has no dander and therefore is an excellent pet for someone with an allergy to the dander in fur. The pig also does not shed, as fur-bearing pets do. The pig will lose strands of hair over time, similar to the way human hair falls out. You can use a brush in a gentle circular motion

If your pig or piglet spends time in a barn, regular grooming is imperative to keep the skin, ears, and eyes free of debris.

to remove loose hair and flaky skin.

EAR CLEANING

Your piggy's ears should be cleaned regularly. If the pig lives with other pets, such as dogs or cats, check the ears regularly for mites. If Rasher—or whatever you have named the family pig—has ear mites, there will be a blackish looking paste in the ear. This is easily treated with mite medication from your vet.

You can clean the pig's ears with a cotton swab and alcohol. Do not get water or liquid in the ear, as it could cause infection. The author recommends having the veterinarian demonstrate proper ear cleaning technique for you before you attempt ear cleaning for the first time. If you do not do it gently and properly, you could injure the ear. Ear cleaning generally is recommended to be done every one to two weeks.

DENTAL HYGIENE

The Pot-Bellied Pig has forty-four teeth. Cleaning should be done regularly by your veterinarian, just as it is for dogs and cats. Also, the pig's "fang" tooth on either side in the front may need to be trimmed, a procedure done by the veterinarian. Follow your pig's veterinarian's advice on any questions concerning the teeth.

HOOF CARE

No, "pickled pig's feet" have nothing to do with your pet piggy's feet. In fact, your Pot-Bellied Pig really does not even have "feet." Your little hoglet has hooves. The hoof is cloven, which means that it is parted or split, as in cattle.

Trimming the Vietnamese Pot-Belly's hooves is quite similar to trimming a dog's nails. In order to make your pig comfortable with this procedure, you should from the very beginning let your piglet get

***Facing page:* Mini pigs have cloven hoofs, which are like two toes. Some people polish the pigs' nails...**

USA

accustomed to the feel of someone touching and working with his hooves.

The dewclaws are easy to trim with dog nail nippers. You should be especially careful not to trim too much. Talk to your baby swine reassuringly while doing the trimming. Be sure to reward your little ham-let afterward with a food treat, a belly rub, or a good affectionate scratching on his sides.

For the main part of the hoof, you can take an emery board and use it around the edge of the

Trimming your pig's hooves are a necessity (like trimming a dog's nails or claws) if they are not naturally worn down. Handle your pig's hooves so it won't be afraid of the grooming process.

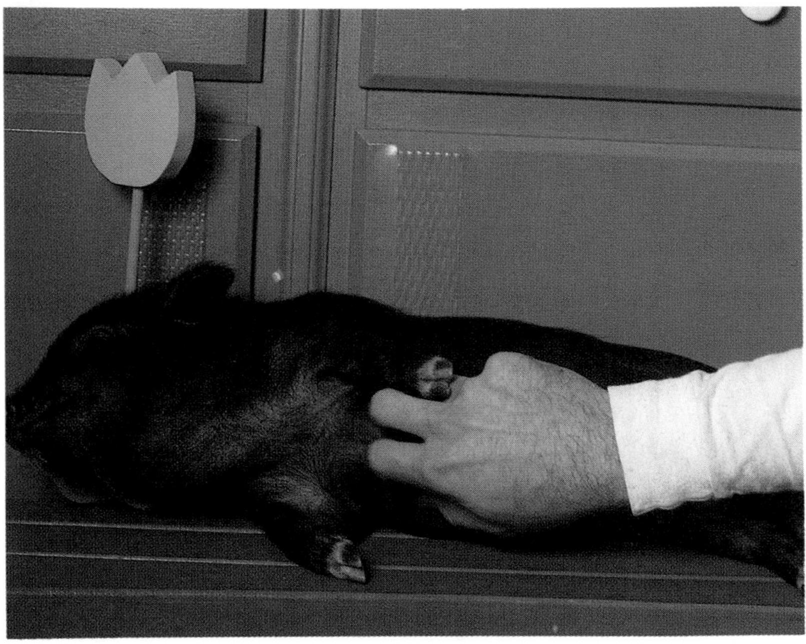

hoof while the pig is young. When the pig gets older, the main part of the hoof can be trimmed using a number ten horse hoof nippers. Gently use the nippers to gradually snip away small increments of the hoof. Then the hoof can be shaped with a flat file. If the pig struggles, STOP or you could injure him. If you are unsure with this procedure, or if your pig will not be still, then it would be best to have your vet do the trimming. If your pig is cared for properly, this procedure should have to be done only once every one and one-half years or so. To condition the hooves, you can use an equine hoof product. The conditioning of the hooves at least once monthly is recommended.

Black polish can be applied to the hooves and buffed for special occasions such as the show ring or photo sessions. You should remember that well-groomed hooves not only make your piggie look more dapper but also are important to proper standing and to the condition of his legs and joints.

HOGWASH!! BATHING YOUR PIG

Excessive bathing can remove the skin's natural oil and dry the skin, and so bathing should only be done when needed. You should not use your own shampoo on your little ham. The pH balance is different, and your shampoo can cause dryness, itching, or skin problems. Instead, use a tearless shampoo product.

Some pigs love water but hate the bathing ritual. Some love the bathing but otherwise hate water. In either case, the best way to bathe your pig indoors is to shut yourself into the shower-tub with him and thus keep him confined until your mission is accomplished. If you start when the pig is tiny and acclimate him gradually to the feel and experience of bathing, he should be very manageable when he is a stout fifty pounds or so. When he is soapy, wet, and slippery, you will be glad that he is calm and manageable rather than squirming.

You should bathe the pig indoors in the winter. In the warm months you can bathe him either indoors or outdoors. After lathering and washing, be sure that your Pot-Belly is rinsed well and that there is no shampoo residue. Then he should be left to dry for about one and one-half hours where there are *no drafts.* His pig house (crate or cage) is one good place for confining him until he dries thoroughly.

After the bathing, you can finish up Miss Piggy's toilette with a mixture of glycerin and water lightly misted over the body. This will make the coat shine. Never put perfume, or any other human cosmetics, on your piggie.

Facing Page: **If you are going to handle your pig in "dress" clothes, you want the animal to be immaculate.**

GROOMING

Keep your pig healthy. Visit your vet regularly.

HEALTH

GOOD PREVENTIVE HEALTH CARE WILL INCLUDE, AMONG OTHER THINGS, PROPER ATTENTION TO HOG HYGIENE, SKIN CARE, EAR CLEANING, HOOF CARE, BATHING, AND DENTAL CARE. WITH PROPER DIET AND GOOD PREVENTIVE HEALTH CARE, YOUR HOUSE PIG CAN HAVE A LIFESPAN BEING ESTIMATED AT UP TO TWENTY TO THIRTY YEARS.

HEALTH AND VETERINARY CARE

(Because the Vietnamese miniatures are still so new, there is not a wealth of literature available on their lifespan, as you might suspect. However, some research has been initiated. For example, California State Polytechnic University in Pomona, California has been studying the Pot-Bellies. As results of various research projects become available over time, we will all be able to learn more about this subject.)

GENERAL HEALTH INFORMATION

The mini pig has a normal body temperature of 103°, which is significantly higher than the human 98.6°. Do not be surprised if the rotund little rascal you have chosen to cohabit with is less tolerant of cold temperatures in his home environment than you are. However, it is interesting that this exotic breed also does not like or do well in extremes of heat. In fact, the Pot-Bellies are notably prone to heat strokes. Never leave your pig in a closed car in summer. Never leave your pig outside on a hot day with no shade. And, never leave your pig without fresh cool water.

It is, in fact, the matter of heat extremes that led to swinekind's undeserved reputation for being dirty animals. Pigs have no sweat glands on their bodies, except for a scattering across the bridge of the nose. They need to "wallow" in water in order to lower the body temperature when they are overheated. If there is no water to wallow in, they will wallow in mud. Hence, the unfair characterization of pigs in general as being filthy, mud-loving beasts.

too. Generally speaking, if the thermometer reads over 85° or under 50° your pig will be uncomfortable. If it is too cold, give your roommate lots of blankets or straw

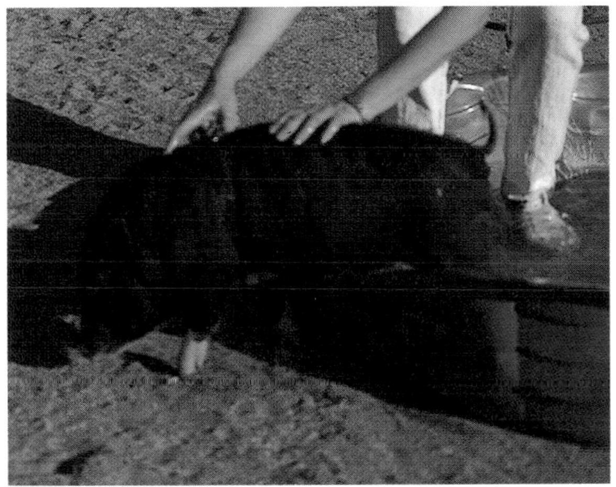

If your pig overheats, or you think it may have overheated, dip him into a swimming pool. A child's wading pool is just fine.

As a rule of thumb, you can gauge your pig's temperature comfort level fairly closely with your own. If you are uncomfortable, then your pug-nosed little quadruped probably is,

to burrow in. There are pet pig owners in Alaska and Canada whose piggies do just fine with the right protection from the cold. If, on the other hand, it is too hot, give your roommate a pool of cool water to play and soak in—or a hosing down with cool water.

Pot-Bellies have a "simple stomach" system, similar to a dog's. Proper feeding for a healthy house pig is not difficult or time-consuming. Neither is it more costly than for a pet dog or cat. (Nutritional requirements for the health and well-being of your pig are covered in the chapter on feeding and nutrition.)

Infant Pot-Bellies should be left with the mother pig (sow) for at least the first three and one-half to four weeks of their lives. If the baby is taken from the mother when it is too young, its health and development can be impaired. If the mother pig has died giving birth (farrowing) or is otherwise not available for the piglets for some reason, they can be bottle-fed. This should not be attempted without competent advice from a veterinarian as to the specific feeding formula content.

Pet Pot-Bellies should not be sold before a minimum age of six weeks. Being moved to new surroundings and having to adjust to a new environment, complete with new people, is very stressful for a baby piglet.

Pot-Bellies reportedly can continue to grow for as long as two years. They are sexually mature at five to seven months of age. Females will grow larger than the males in this breed. Also, the female reportedly will grow larger in size with each litter that she farrows.

The male piglet can be neutered in the first few weeks of his life. If the male is neutered

Pot-Bellies should not be purchased before they are six weeks old.

(castrated) before his full maturity, he is called a barrow in the parlance of pig-dom. A male pig neutered after reaching his full maturity is a stag. A mature unaltered male is a boar. If your house pig is a male and you do not intend to use him for breeding, then you most definitely should have him neutered. Otherwise, you will most certainly find that having a boar as a house companion is not "hog heaven." It is the nature of the species that the boar is quite malodorous. There is a foul odor about him—his breath, his body, his urine, etc.—that is rather akin to sulfurous rotten eggs. Also, the boar will be more aggressive in his disposition.

If your pet Pot-Belly is a female, then in the language of swineologists she is referred to as a gilt if she has never had a litter. If she has had a litter, then she is a sow. An open sow is one that is not currently bred. The female Pot-Belly will have her first heat at five to seven months of age. The heat, which lasts for one to five days, will cycle approximately every twenty-one days until the pig is bred. The typical litter for a Pot-Belly mini pig is about six piglets. A sow can have two litters per year without there being undue stress to her, but more than two is not recommended. As it is, the life expectancy of the sows is projected to be less than other pigs precisely because of the stresses of having offspring, or farrowing.

If you should become

***Facing Page:* Pot-Bellies are naturally curious...but this one is crazy about television!**

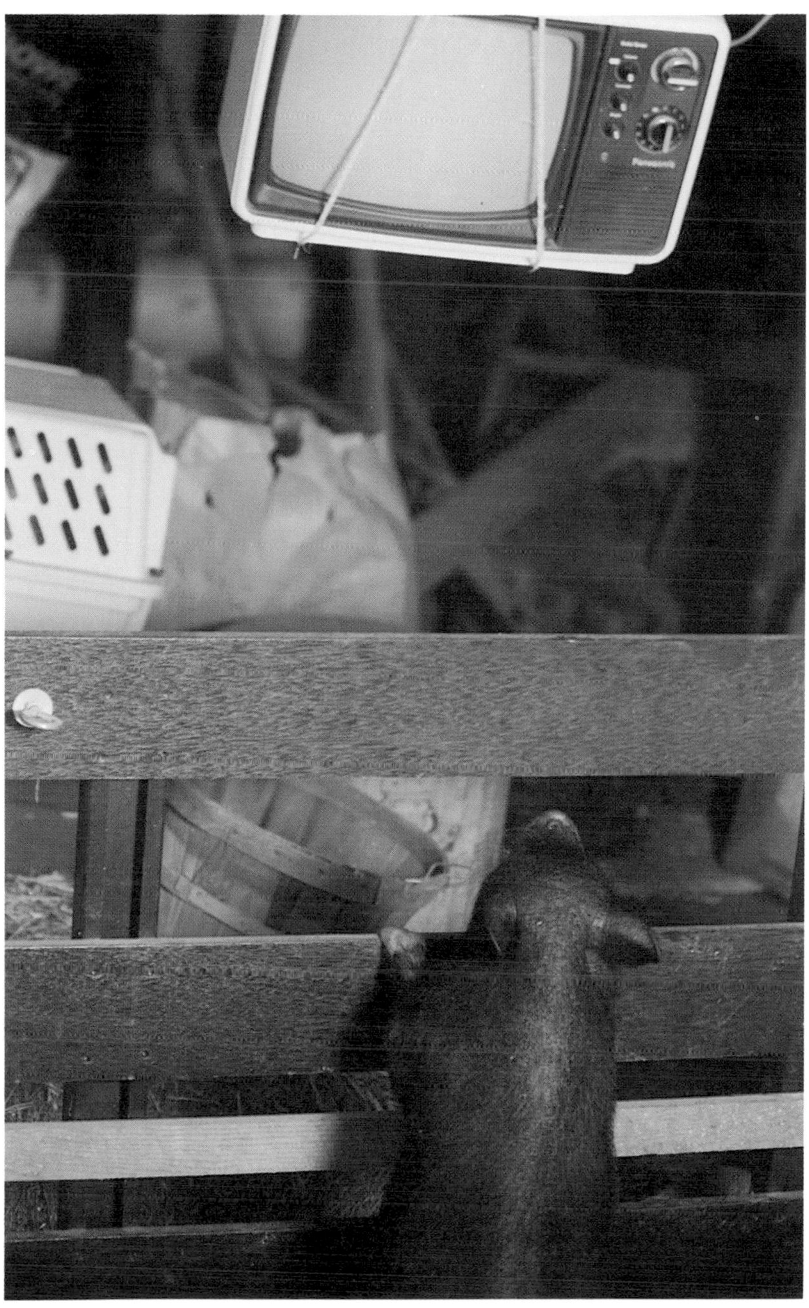

interested in breeding these adorable ungainly-looking pot-bellied critters, then you will want to get detailed information on the factors associated with mortality and morbidity in baby pigs, and other pertinent pig health information. However, we will not attempt to go into that detail within the scope of this book.

VACCINATIONS

Check with your veterinarian regarding your pet pig's vaccination requirements. The following list is presented as a general reference to vaccinations that are presently available:

(I) Swivax 8. A vaccine against *Erysipelothrix*, leptospirosis, parvovirus, and *Pasteurella* A and D.

(2) Bordagea P/D. A vaccine against *Bordetella* and *Pasteurella* A and D.

(3) Litterguard. A vaccine against *Clostridium perfringens* type C and *E. coli.*

(4) Porsivac PV5L. A five-way vaccination.

COMMON AILMENTS AND HEALTH PROBLEMS

Hog cholera, a disease of epidemic proportions prevalent in farm pigs some decades ago, fortunately has been virtually eliminated in the United States now. Today there are no reported diseases that you as a human species can catch from your mini pig species—i.e., nothing that is contagious to humans.

Also, the Pot-Bellies normally do not have fleas, ticks, mites, or mange, assuming they are kept in a clean environment.

There are a number of diseases or ailments that

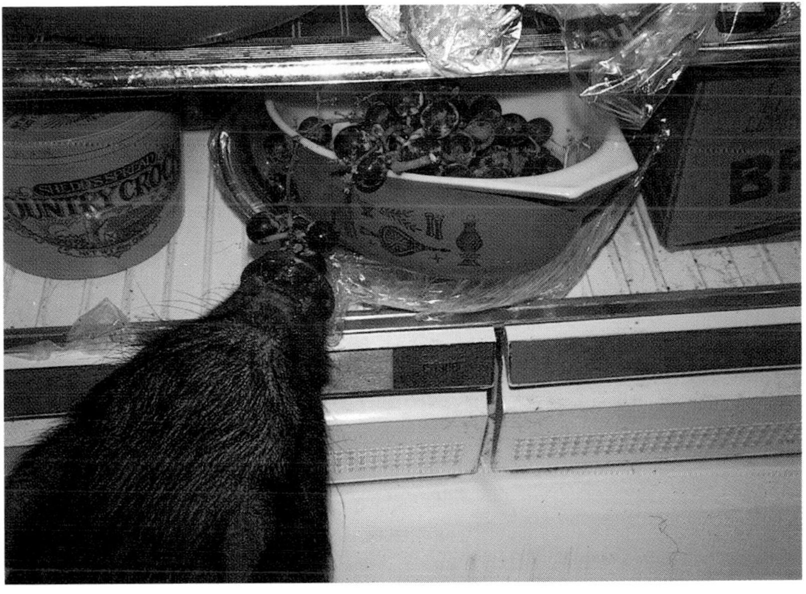

Can you imagine what would happen if your mini pig learned to open your refrigerator door?

may affect your portly little swine. They will be covered only briefly here. Please always consult your veterinarian immediately if you notice any change in your piggy's behavior, appetite and eating habits, or physical condition. Atrophic rhinitis is a viral infection of the snout. Another potential cause of respiratory symptoms or problems is allergies, which some pigs may be susceptible to. Swine flu is a viral respiratory infection that is highly contagious to other pigs. It is important to know this if you have more than one pet Pot-Belly in your home. Mycoplasmal pneumonia is another respiratory infection type.

E. coli is an ailment that causes baby pig scours, which is diarrhea. Scours is not common in adult pigs. Bloody diarrhea is another condition that would require your vet's attention.

Porcine parvovirus is an intestinal inflammation. One long-term disease is pasteurellosis, a bacterial infection. Erysipelas refers to a bacterial infection commonly contracted from stress or from other pigs.

Haemophilus pleuropneumoniae is another type of bacterial infection. Leptospirosis is a kidney infection. One viral disease, transmissible gastroenteritis, is passed from the sow to her piglets.

Rickets results from poor diet. Another diet-related health problem in pigs is hypoglycemia, which is low blood sugar.

Parasites that you might encounter with your pig include ascarids (roundworm), lice, fly maggots, and mites. Again, mange is not common with Pot-Bellies. If it should occur, one suggested treatment is to wash the affected area with a gentle formula skin cleaner.

The exotic mini pigs are susceptible to weak ankles, as well as to arthritis. It is important that your pet's bedding be especially thick and fluffy—like bed comforters—to provide a soft, cushiony support for his bones.

The Vietnamese Pot-Bellied Pig also is prone to strokes, heart attacks, and heat stroke. As previously mentioned, a pig has no sweat glands, except for the few across the bridge of his nose. He can dehydrate very rapidly. The availability of cool, fresh water at all times is crucial. This includes water to soak in and cool his skin in warm weather, as well as drinking water.

Excess weight is a common health problem for pigs. The control and maintenance of a proper diet for your pet is essential to prevent obesity. A pig can get so fat, in fact, that the fat bulges around his face will prevent him from opening his eyes.

If you live in a cold climate and your pig goes outside at all, then hypothermia and frostbite are potential dangers to your pig. Do not leave him outside unattended for more than a few minutes at a time.

Injury is another

Pot-Bellies are susceptible to sunstroke. Keep them out of the sun as much as possible.

category of health concern for your piggy. Leg injuries are particularly common. Do not put your pig up on a table or counter, such that he could jump or fall from that height and injure his legs. Also, do not put a piglet in a child's playpen or any other type of enclosure where he could catch his dewclaw or leg between the rails and thus injure himself. One other major hazard for potential injury to your pig is dogs. Never leave your piglet or pig unattended outside if there are loose neighborhood dogs that could get to him.

HOW TO GIVE MEDICATIONS AT HOME

Pills can be stuffed into one of your pig's favorite treat foods—a grape, a small bit of fruit, a small chunk of bread or roll. This ruse will probably work initially. However, your piggy more than likely will catch on to this trick fairly quickly. Then you can expect to see your little wise guy "sort" the food out in his mouth, swallow what he wants, and spit out the pill.

If your pig cannot be duped into taking a pill, you will have to force him or her to take it. Your best approach is probably to have one person hold the pig, while the other half of the team tilts the head back, opens the mouth, and inserts the pill way back to the throat. Be careful to try to keep your fingers from between an upper and lower jaw that are closing together. The pig's teeth are sharp. Have your veterinarian demonstrate the best technique(s) for administering pills. Over time, you will discover which method works best for your pet.

If the medication is in powder form, you can try mixing it with food or in some fruit juice. Again, follow your veterinarian's advice in this area.

STATE HEALTH REQUIREMENTS

Some states, like Kentucky, require that all mini pigs be tested for brucellosis and pseudo rabies. Check with your veterinarian to determine your own state's laws and specific health requirements for pet pigs, as this does vary from state to state.

CLIPPING OF EYE TEETH

Clipping of the eye teeth, or "fang" teeth, on baby piglets seems to be a fairly standard procedure. Some suggest clipping the eye teeth right after birth. This is a procedure that must be done carefully to avoid injury to the piglet. Do not attempt it yourself unless you have been educated by a veterinarian as to the proper way to do this.

SUNBURN

If your pet Pot-Belly is left outside without shade, he can be sunburned. More particularly, he can be subject to a condition called photosensitization, which affects pigs and which you should be watchful for with your Pot-Belly.

If you should observe your pet pig to be oozing fluids from his ears, back, or other areas after some exposure to the sun, your veterinarian's immediate attention is recommended.

Generally speaking, it

appears that in the long run the mini pig is a relatively hardy pet. You will probably find that your pet pig is at least as healthy as the more typical house pets and is no more costly to maintain with respect to his veterinary care.

Your mini pig will cost you just as much as a dog in terms of annual veterinarian bills....but it's worth it!

BOARDING

IF YOU PLAN TO DO ANY TRAVELLING FOR BUSINESS OR VACATIONS, YOU BASICALLY HAVE THREE OPTIONS WITH RESPECT TO YOUR PETS, INCLUDING YOUR PET PIG. THE CHOICES ARE:

(1) TAKE THE PIG WITH YOU.

(2) BOARD THE PIG AT A KENNEL, VETERINARIAN'S OFFICE, OR ONE OF THE

This is a good-quality Pot-Belly. Note the stand-up ears, straight tail, and good ratio of height to length.

"HOG SITTING" OR BOARDING YOUR MINI PIG

more luxurious "pet resorts."

(3) Have someone come in and "hog sit" at your home.

It may be a personal quirk, but the author does not favor option one for any pet. At best, travelling is not a pleasant or comfortable experience for your pet. At worst, travelling can subject him to motion sickness, drafts and temperature changes, disease, stress, and the danger of getting loose and lost in a strange place.

Option two is superior to option one, although it has drawbacks, too. Many boarding facilities will not take pigs. Boarding means unfamiliar surroundings, which is stressing to the pig. Pigs, like most other pets, prefer the familiarity and stability of home.

If you must board your pig, the following guidelines are suggested for the health and welfare of your pig:

(1) Board with a veterinarian, if possible, or with a facility that has a veterinarian on call. Someone trained in medical care should be available to notice if your pig seems ill or listless.

(2) Be sure the facility takes precautions against diseases and that the other animals being boarded appear to be healthy and comfortable.

(3) Be sure the facility has experience with pigs. If they do not, educate the personnel who will be caring for your pig with explicit verbal and written instructions.

(4) Leave a number where you can be reached, and the number for your piggy's regular veterinarian.

The best course of action for the piggy's sake is the third option. Make arrangements in advance. Have the

Pigs get along with puppies better than puppies get along with pigs.

(5) Leave your pig's blanket, one or two favorite toys, and anything else familiar that will make your pig feel more reassured while you are gone.

(6) Leave any needed medications, with instructions.

neighbor, friend, or hired sitter come in before you leave so that you can introduce the sitter to the pig. The pig will be reassured to see that you know this person, and will sense through you that the sitter is "okay." Be sure that the sitter is not afraid of the pig, either.

Leave the same special food, medications, and instructions that you would leave if you were boarding the pig. In addition to the regular pig diet that you would leave when boarding your pig, you can leave more "treat" foods at home for your homebound friend. For example, you can leave lettuce and pieces of fruit cut up in the refrigerator for the sitter to give to your appreciative piggy.

Whether your pig is housebroken to use a litter box or to go outside, leave instructions as to the routine he is accustomed to. Also, do not forget your pig's sensitivity to temperature extremes. Wherever you leave him should be climate controlled to remain within the pig's comfort range.

Having a pet pig at home does not mean that you must be "hog tied." You can travel. Having a pig, however, does mean that you will have to plan to make careful arrangements for your companion, just as you should for any other pet.

PERSONALITY

YOUR PYGMOID (MINIATURE) PIG PLAYMATE PROBABLY WILL, FOR STARTERS, EXPECT TO BE TREATED MORE LIKE A FAMILY MEMBER THAN A PET. THE GREAT SIR WINSTON CHURCHILL ONCE MADE THE OBSERVATION THAT DOGS LOOK UP TO US, CATS LOOK DOWN ON US, BUT PIGS TREAT US AS EQUALS. AND, LIKE ANY

PORCINE PERSONALITY— THE BEHAVIOR OF YOUR PYGMY PIG

other family member, your pygmy pal will exhibit a spectrum of behaviors that range from those that amuse you to those that annoy you. Please do not expect him to be perfect. After all, no one else in your family is, are they?

GENERAL BEHAVIOR CHARACTERISTICS

Intelligence is probably a good place to start, because your pig is packed with it. Although there will always be some debate on which animals are brighter than which others, the *general* ranking attributed to the pig for a considerable number of years now is fourth. The only species reputed to be brighter by those who are expert in such things are (in rank order): humans, chimps/ apes, whales and dolphins. If you doubt it, go ahead and ask the next ethologist or zoologist you run into at a cocktail party.

If you ask a person who has both dogs and mini pigs (as this author has in a good number of instances) to tell you which he thinks is smarter, the answer is invariably the pig. The pig learns commands and tricks more quickly. The pig is housebroken as easily or more easily than the dog. Like the dog, the pig can be trained in regular obedience classes.

For all that you will find the pig compared with the dog—intelligence, training methods, learning patterns and behaviors—

there is one aspect of the diminutive mini pig's intelligence that goes beyond the boundary of what is comparable to the dog. The pig is *shrewd,* as well. In this regard, you will probably find him more like a young child.

By way of example, assume that you have just disciplined your pet dog for something by some routine yelling, a mild swat on his rump, and sending him to stay in a corner of the living room as penance. The dog will obey, slink to the corner guiltily, promptly forget the whole episode, and probably fall sound asleep. Now, assume the same hypothetical discipline for your pet pig. The pig will also obey. However, far from demonstrating "guilt" in his demeanor, he will probably squeal in angry frustration at being disciplined—and he will *not* promptly forget the whole episode. Instead, you will probably observe him lying in the same corner with a switching tail and a murderous look of unmistakable rage in his beady little eyes as he plots some type of "revenge" for you. The calculating "thinking" that is going on in the pig's mind can be read in his eyes, his body language, and his "pouting" attitude just as with a child. And—also just as with a child—you will probably find some time later that he has done something "naughty" to "get even" and vent his anger (shred up some paper, maybe).

The pig's shrewdness is not limited simply to vengeance plots, either. Again, with behavior like a mirror image of an endearing young child, your bristly, rumpled-looking pet also can be devious and sneaky.

Humans who live with pigs report that they will "sneak" to do what they know is forbidden. For example, they will sneak to harass the dog or the cat when the owner is in another room. One owner describes the ritual that her pet Pot-Belly goes through in order not to get caught stealing food. First, the pig goes to the room where she knows there is food that she is not supposed to have. Knowing that if the owner passes by in the hallway and sees the pig in that room, she will be chastised, the pig therefore sneaks into the room as quietly as possible and then slowly, noiselessly pushes the door to that room closed behind her. Amazingly, the pig has "reasoned" that if the owner happens to go by in the hall, she will not be caught by the owner if she is (a) deliberately quiet, and (2) not visible from the hall because the door is closed.

There are equally as many stories from owners who have tried, on the other hand, to be similarly devious or otherwise outsmart their pig. If you think you can trick your pig—in order to catch him, give him medication, or some other such scenario—be prepared for a true challenge. If you do succeed and trip your pig up once, he very likely will remember it and never be fooled by the same trick again. He is wily, and he catches on very swiftly.

The fact that the pet pig is wily and shrewd, as well as merely intelligent, is part of his charm. If you can appreciate this and find humor in this aspect of his porcine personality, you will enjoy the challenge of sharing your home with him just that much more. If you feel that you would not enjoy this type of personality, then please consider some other type of pet. Neither you nor the pig will be happy or do one another justice.

While recognizing that pigs are probably MENSA candidates relative to the rest of us creatures in the food chain, we should also note that they *can* be duped, given the right circumstances. Hunters in colonial times in the United States used an interesting ploy. They carved life-sized decoy wooden pigs to attract wild boar. The early decoys were often made of an entire tree, and were quite cumbersome. Later *artistes de hog* (pig carvers) discovered that smaller scale versions seemed to fool the boar more effectively than the earlier, larger decoys.

It seems that the myopic (near-sighted) swine believed the smaller decoys to be other wild pigs in the distance.

Other general behavior traits include the following, some of which you will like and some of which you may not:

- Easily housebroken
- Pigheaded—i.e., obstinate or stubborn
- "Boss Hog"— will try to dominate other pets, especially dogs

TRAINING

NEVER TRY TO TEACH A PIG TO SING. IT WASTES YOUR TIME, AND IT ANNOYS THE PIG—UNKNOWN.

THE SUBJECT OF TRAINING COULD—AND PROBABLY SHOULD—HAVE A SEPARATE, ENTIRE BOOK DEVOTED TO IT ALONE. THIS CHAPTER, NECESSARILY, CAN PROVIDE ONLY A FAIRLY BRIEF AND GENERAL COVERAGE OF THIS

Training your pig to walk on a lead is simple. It can also be trained to do other 'tricks.'

TRAINING YOUR PET

important topic, but you are advised to explore on your own and learn as much as you can. Sources of information on animal training in general can be helpful. Also, some pig owners enroll their pigs in dog obedience training classes. You can consider doing this, or at least talk with the trainers who conduct the obedience training to see if they could customize some training for your pig. It is not really that dissimilar from dog training. Actually, it is probably most like a combination of the principles of dog training together with the principles of young child training.

THE FIRST CARDINAL RULE OF PIG TRAINING

This is actually the author's first rule of training any animal, including your pig. It is: "Train the Human First." There normally is no problem with training that cannot be traced to one of two causes. Those are:

(1) The animal is sick or stressed.

(2) The human "trainer" is doing something wrong or confusing to the animal in the training.

Whether symptomatic of cause number one or number two, the problem's resolution rests with the human, not the animal. Blaming your pet, or expecting him to correct the underlying cause of the problem, is unfair and is expecting him to do the impossible.

An example of a cause number one situation was a friend with a wonderful house cat who asked if the author could suggest why this new cat had used the litter box initially but then had started to urinate on the carpet and on the bed. Diagnosing the problem was not difficult when the author went to her home. The kitty's box was a mess. The friend confessed that she thought changing the box every seven to ten days would be sufficient. The poor cat was so repulsed by the unclean box that she was forced to use other places, and also was becoming ill from stress and cystitis from trying to "hold" her urine.

An example of the cause number two situation is the pet owner who wonders why his pet pig will not come to him so that he can, for example, give the pig his medicine. The reason nearly always is that the owner has done that in the past and the pig is now afraid to come when called. *Never* call your pig to come to you and then do something distasteful to him—discipline, medication, bathing, a trip to the veterinarian, etc. If you must do something unpleasant, simply go and get the pig. Let your piggy always associate coming to you in response to your call with pleasant things, such as treats, praise, scratching, petting, or playing.

The cause number two situation is very common. If you observe any dog obedience classes, you will see that much of the

Like training any other animal, pig training requires time and patience.

training actually is directed at the humans present. The humans are not there simply because their dogs happened to need a ride to and from the class. They are there to be "trained" too—to learn how to work with their pets.

THE SECOND CARDINAL RULE OF PIG TRAINING

This rule is: "Punishment, especially corporal punishment, is *never* necessary."

Discipline is necessary. However, physical pain or punishment is not.

Regarding discipline, remember that you cannot discipline your pig unless you catch him or her in the act. Otherwise, the pig will not associate the discipline with the act. Discipline can be done with a stern, scolding voice, and perhaps shaking your finger in the pig's face. The pig does understand facial expressions and the intonation of your voice, and your little porker will understand your disappointment just as well as if you had struck him. The effect of your saying "No" firmly also can be intensified, if necessary, by accompanying it with a squirt from a water pistol. Discipline involving hands on the pig is okay if it involves, say, shoving or pushing, as to push him away from the refrigerator, for example, but never hitting or beating.

Ralph Helfer, who ranks among the world's foremost animal trainers, created and uses "affection training" with his animals. The hundreds of wild animals that he has trained for films and television are clearly excellent examples of the fact that there is no need for the use of pain or fear in the training of any animal.

Training your piggy requires—as with any other animal—lots of patience, persistence, and praise. Use praise and small treats as rewards for correct responses and correct behavior. If you establish a foundation of love, approval, mutual respect, and rewards in combination with clear and appropriate discipline, then you and your house pig will live in harmony.

Many' of the Pot-Belly mini piglets have already been given "basic training" when they are sold, at least to the extent that they have been housebroken. If you must housebreak your new family addition, then you can either:

(1) Follow the instructions given to you by the pet store or breeder that sold you the piglet. Many sellers have a package of information, with detailed instructions for housebreaking, that comes to you with your new baby bundle of joy.

(2) Follow the standard instructions for kitten housebreaking (there are lots of manuals, guides, pamphlets, etc. for this) if you plan to use a litter box. One difference is that for piggies you can use cedar shavings or newspaper shreddings.

(3) Follow the standard instructions for puppy or dog housebreaking (there are lots of manuals, guides, pamphlets, etc. for this, too) if you plan to train your oinker to relieve himself outside.

Your pet pig easily can be trained to the harness and leash. Start your pig as young as possible, preferably eight to ten weeks. Use a dog harness and lead until your pig is about six

Facing page: **Never use force or punish a pig with physical contact. Training is a slow, deliberate, gradual process.**

months old. At that time he will be close enough to full grown that a good adjustable pig harness will work from then on. The harness should be of a soft material, such as cotton. Nylon or leather may irritate the pig's skin. If you notice any irritation, discontinue using that particular type of harness.

For the initial leash training, put the harness on and leave it on for gradually more extended periods of time. When the pig is used to the feel, add the leash and let him drag that around the house to accustom him to it before ever going outside. Train as you would a puppy, with commands of "come" or "stay," using treats as rewards.

For training in general, it is advisable to start as young as possible. The older pig is harder to train, as he is more stubborn and independent. The adult swine will be less willing to do what you want him or her to do. Also, do not train a baby pig to do anything you do not want him to do when adult. The piglet may be cute sitting on your sofa, but if you do not want the forty-pound adult to be sharing your sofa then do not let the baby pig do so. It is more difficult to un-train or re-train your pig than to train him properly in the first place.

Never force your pig to do anything, especially if it is something he fears. Pigs do not respond to ultimatums or force and in fact are more likely to do just the opposite of what you want if you try to force them. Be patient, let the pig develop his trust, and let him work at his own pace.

TRAINING

Following is a list of the types of things that mini pigs have been trained to do:

- •Harness and leash training
- •Give kisses
- •Wear clothes (swine finery)
- •Ring bell when ready to go outside (housebreaking)
- •Growl or "bark" when ready to come back inside
- •Pirouette
- •Do figure eights through the owner's legs
- •Use "piggy door" to go outside
- •Drink from a soft drink can
- •Come when called
- •Shake "hands"
- •Stay
- •Climb stairs

Lena Molokova and Galya Gerasimova at the school pig farm of the "Chernopensky" collective farm in Russia, 1991, with their mini-pig.

BREEDING

IF YOU THINK THAT YOU MIGHT WANT TO BRANCH OUT FROM THE SIMPLE ONE-PIG HOUSEHOLD TO THE BREEDING AND RAISING OF PET PIGS, THINK IT OVER AT LEAST TWICE. IT IS NOT EASY. PLEASE DO NOT TRY TO DO IT UNLESS YOU ARE FULLY PREPARED TO DO IT RIGHT.

THERE ARE TOO MANY "BACKYARD BREEDERS,"

BREEDING AND RAISING MINIATURE PIGS

unfortunately, who erroneously believe that setting up and operating a piggery is a snap. Breeding and raising should be done only by those who are thoroughly knowledgeable and are ethically responsible to the species. There is quite a significant dollar investment involved, not only for the right breeding stock but also for the right kind of facilities. There is a significant labor investment, as well; recognize that this involves hard work. Anyone who views the pigs as "breeding machines" and puts the consideration of making money ahead of the pigs' well-being and welfare has no place in this business and would be well advised to look into another type of venture.

Female pigs can go into heat from about age five months on. It is generally recommended not to breed until the pig is a minimum of seven to eight months of age. The heat cycle is every twenty-one days, and lasts from three to five days, typically.

Artificial insemination is one of the breeding options. It is recommended as being both cheaper and safer for the pig. The female Pot-Belly tends to grow larger in size with each litter that she farrows, a uniquely interesting characteristic of these porcine house pets. Gestation is three months, three weeks, and three days—or, one hundred and fourteen days.

Pigs usually tend to be good mothers and are very protective of the baby piglets. However, special attention is called for at the time of the birth. If left unattended, a new mother pig can, for example, inadvertently injure or kill her piglets by stepping on them. For other reasons, as well, the early care of the neonatal (newborn) piglets is particularly critical to their survival. It is important that any breeder be knowledgeable and competent in the difficult area of neonatal pig care and that there be a veterinarian on call during the critical neonatal period in case of problems.

Pigs are lactating mammals, which means that the young are nursed by the mother. A newborn piglet will weigh less than one pound and fit in the palm of your hand. It is recommended for the sow's health that she have no more than a maximum of two litters per year.

If you are considering the breeding and raising of mini pet pigs, you should seek detailed information on these subjects from your veterinarian, NAPPA, one of the registry services, or some other such expert source.

BREEDING

There is a 'law' of nature which goes something like this: 'Garbage in; garbage out'. This not only applies to breeding pigs, but it applies to computer science, book writing and many other things. You only need a female to breed pigs. You can always 'rent' a male or even use some artificial insemination techniques in order to impregnate your female and start a piggery. Pigs are excellent mothers.

THE LAW

IF YOU HAVE DECIDED THAT YOU ARE "HOG-TIED" TO THE IDEA OF SHARING YOUR HOME WITH ONE OF THESE PORTLY PORCINE CRITTERS, THEN PLEASE DO THE NECESSARY RESEARCH FIRST TO DETERMINE IF YOU WILL BE ALLOWED TO KEEP THE PIG AS A HOUSE PET WITH NO PROBLEMS. CONTACT YOUR STATE'S FISH AND GAME

YOUR MINI PIG AND THE LAW

department and/or wildlife commission, as well as the appropriate local zoning authorities. Some states and residential areas have stricter laws than others.

Generally, you will not find the Pot-Bellied Miniature Pig specifically referred to in most any legislation or ordinances. They are still too new.

Usually, if the animal is considered "wildlife," you will find that there may be laws that prohibit keeping or possessing the animal. If the animal is considered to be "livestock," then zoning ordinances may prohibit the keeping of the animal. Most cities, for example, bar pigsties and swineries. However, if the animal is considered an "exotic pet," then generally laws would permit the keeping of one or more as house pets. The operative phraseology relative to an "exotic pet" is usually in the nature of "not native to the state" and "to be kept only for personal enjoyment or companionship."

With the advent of the mini pig craze, many city council bodies are being petitioned to amend their ordinances to specifically allow pet Pot-Bellies to live in the city and residential areas. It is important to be aware, though, that an amendment allowing pet pigs would not include the breeding and raising of the pigs if you are within city limits. A piggery would be viewed as a commercial operation and probably would require agricultural zoning or other special zoning.

Where laws are mute on the new mini pigs, it appears that they are usually treated like other pets, such as cats and dogs. However, it is best to be safe and research your own area's laws to be sure that you will have no complications. Please make certain that your new little pet piglet is excluded from your state's legal definition of "wildlife," and that zoning does not pose a potential legal issue.

Also, it may be prudent to do a little campaigning in your neighborhood before you "bring home the bacon." The enforcement of zoning ordinances is nearly always based on a complaint from a neighbor. If you explain your pet to your neighbors and let them know that he is not going to be a negative factor to the neighborhood, you may prevent any future complaining influences.

In fact, from the perspective of neighbors, a mini pig should in many ways be preferable to dogs. They do not bark. They are not malodorous. They do not bite. They do not fight. And, they do not run loose or run in packs, as dogs often do.

CELEBRITY PIGS

MANKIND ADORES SWINEKIND. THIS HAS BEEN OBVIOUS THROUGH THE DECADES. WE ALL REMEMBER THE BELOVED CELEBRITY PIGS FROM THE CARTOONS THAT WE GREW UP WITH: PORKY PIG AND PETUNIA. MISS PIGGY, ANOTHER TREASURED PIG PERSONALITY AND STAR, WAS THE MUPPET CREATION OF THE LATE JIM HENSON.

"HAMMING IT UP"—CELEBRITY PIGS

If you watch any rerun of the television sitcom *Green Acres,* you cannot fail to notice the wonderful Arnold. Arnold, of course, was a "farm pig," a much larger cousin of the Pot-Bellied miniatures. Arnold also made appearances on other television programs, such as *The Tonight Show.*

Penelopy Pitstop, a black Pot-Belly who lives with Flame Beller, is the mascot for a radio station in Phoenix, Arizona. A pig of great porcine pulchritude, "Nellie" never misses a photo opportunity and enjoys being dressed up for special events and appearances. Arnold, a Pot-Belly who belongs to Kiyoko Hancock in California, was the photo-pig for *Vogue* magazine when *Vogue* selected the Pot-Bellied Pig as Pet of the Month in August 1990. The photogenic Arnold also appears in much of Kiyoko Hancock's piggy literature, her "Pig Tale Times" newsletter, and other piggy promotional material.

There is no miniature pig who is yet counted among the elite celebrity animal super-stars of films and television. However, with the mini pigs' high intelligence and great adaptability to training, the author expects that that level of stardom will come to pass in the not-too-distant future.

Reportedly, the American Humane Association, sponsor of

the now-defunct Patsy Awards, plans to revive that very popular event soon. The Patsy Award is the equivalent of the Academy Awards for performing animal stars. If this wonderful event is reestablished, we may soon see one of the Vietnamese mini "hams" hamming it up to a Patsy Award. A miniature "Hamlet" would be a delightful addition to the animal superstars of stage and screen.

March 1st has been proclaimed National Pig Day in the United States. That means that on at least one day every year, pet pigs in the U.S. are celebrities, with a national day in their honor. This day of recognition was started "to accord to the pig its rightful, though generally unrecognized, place as one of man' s most intellectual and useful domesticated animals."

The love of mankind for "swinekind" is evident in all the various forms of art and entertainment — films, television, literature, song, paintings, sculpture, ceramics and pottery, poetry, and so on.

In literature, one beloved pig story has become a classic. *Charlotte's Web,* E. B. White's 1952 fable, is the story of an innocent piglet, Wilbur, who is befriended by a wise arachnid named Charlotte. The gentle Wilbur, as the story unfolds, was born to be fattened for the butcher's cleaver. Charlotte, abetted in her spider's plot by a rat named Templeton, devises a plan to save Wilbur by making him more valuable alive than as a meal in this endearing classic.

PRODUCTS

PRODUCTS FOR PET PIGS RANGE FROM THE PRACTICAL TO THE PRECOCIOUS—FROM NUTRITION ITEMS TO FASHIONABLE "PIGWEAR." NEW PRODUCTS AND SERVICES SEEM TO BE SPRINGING UP ALMOST DAILY. THIS SECTION IS NOT ALL-INCLUSIVE, BUT IT WILL GIVE YOU A GOOD IDEA OF THE TYPES OF RESOURCES

PET PIG RESOURCES AND PRODUCTS

available for your pig-related questions and the types of products for your pet.

Pot-Bellied Pigs magazine, published by the Sarnan company, premiered in October 1990. Subscription information:

Sarnan Publishing
P.O. Box 853
Ooltewah, Tennessee 37363

The Piggie Bank is a newsletter for pig enthusiasts, published by John and Linda Bickel. Subscription information:

The Piggie Bank
15650 North River Road
Alva, Florida 33920

Manual for Potbellied Pig Owners and Breeders is a handbook available from *The Piggie Bank* (address above) that deals with how to profitably breed and raise Pot-Bellies.

Registry Services—The major ones are covered in the chapter on registration and registry services. The registries also can be contacted for other pig-related services and products that they variously offer.

Professional training and handling lessons and consultation services for mini pigs are offered by:

Susan and Chuck Conway
P.O.Box 1837
Grass Valley, California 95949

North American Potbelly Pig Association (NAPPA)—Contact the registry services for information on scheduled meetings and activities. Also, there are local pig clubs and groups that have formed across the United States.

Pig Hotline: 415-879-0061 (Kiyoko and Co.) Any type of pet pig-related questions can be directed to this hotline.

Miniature Pot-Bellied Pig First Time Buyer's Guide is a softcover guide by A. K. Garrett that discusses the pros and cons of owning a Pot-Bellied Pig and what to do when you get yours home. Published by JRAK Enterprises, Parker, CO.

Pot-Bellied Pet Pigs: Mini-Pig Care and Training is a softcover guide written by Kayla Mull and Lorrie Blackburn, D.V.M. (All Publishing, Orange, CA) Published in 1989, it covers what *not* to teach your pet pig, as well as what to teach him, and it suggests various training techniques suited to the Pot-Belly.

Pigg-EE Palace, owned by Flame Beller, is a product distribution venture for pig-related products. Started early in 1989, this source has as wide a range of items for the pig-mania people as you could expect to find anywhere. Products include custom-made halters and pig-wear, made of materials that will not rub or irritate the pig's skin. Products have been shipped to Europe, Australia, and other corners of the world to swinophiles. The Pigg-EE Palace enterprise also operates an adoption service for abandoned or mistreated piggies. The address is:

Pigg-EE Palace
P.O. Box 43556
Phoenix, AZ 85080-3556

INDEX

POT-BELLIED PIGS
and other Miniature Pet Pigs

Lisa Hall Huckaby

TS-181